LONGMAN

D0808424

Classic English

Students' Book with Workbook

by

◄ *Robert O'Neill*

with
Gaynor Ramsey

Contents

1

Hello!

 This is Susan Farr.

And this is Bernard Winter.

"Hello. My name is Susan Farr."

"Hello. My name is Bernard Winter."

What about you? What's your name?

1 Listen and read.

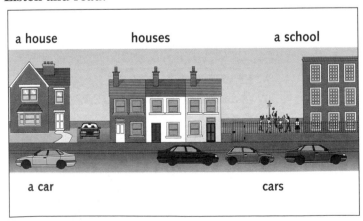

a house   houses   a school

a car   cars

Names

Bernard Susan Diana

a man   a woman

Vocabulary

2 Look.

Numbers

1 one	4 four	7 seven
2 two	5 five	8 eight
3 three	6 six	9 nine

✔ yes   ✗ no

3 Say the number. Then say the word.

One. **1** *A man.*   **2** *A woman.*

3 *A telephone.*   **4** *A clock.*

4 Say the telephone numbers.

oh two three one
five nine oh seven four eight

1   **0231 590748**

2   **0907 621503**   *oh nine oh seven...*

3   **0698 249484**

4   **0463 303709**

5   **0505 829070**

5 What time is it?

Question	Answer
What time is it?	*It's... o'clock.*

1   2   3

4   5   6

6 Answer the questions.

Question   **Answer**

Is that a house?   *Yes.*

Is that a school?   *No.*

1 Is that a telephone?
2 Is it a clock?
3 Is it four o'clock?

4 Is that a clock?
5 Is it a telephone?
6 Is that your
   telephone number?

Pronunciation

7 Listen and say the words.

1 sch<u>oo</u>l, tw<u>o</u>
2 n<u>o</u>, teleph<u>o</u>ne
3 wh<u>a</u>t, cl<u>o</u>ck
4 f<u>i</u>ve, t<u>i</u>me, m<u>y</u>
5 n<u>a</u>me, <u>ei</u>ght

Classic Extra page 94

2

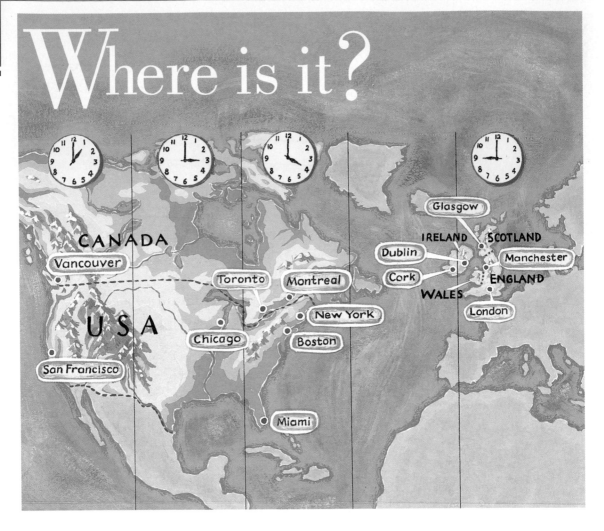

Where is it?

The United States is a country. Canada is a country, too.

New York is a city in the United States. Toronto is a city, too. It isn't in the United States. Toronto is in Canada.

San Francisco and Boston are in the United States. Boston is near New York. San Francisco isn't near New York.

It is one o'clock in San Francisco and four o'clock in New York. In London it is nine o'clock.

England is a small country but London is a big city. Oxford is near London.

Dublin is in Ireland. Edinburgh is in Scotland. Glasgow is in Scotland, too.

1 Answer the questions.

1 What time is it in Toronto?
2 Where is Montreal?
3 Is Scotland a big country?
4 Where is Chicago?
5 What time is it in San Francisco?

2 What about you?

1 Are you in a big city now?
2 What time is it there?
3 What country are you in?
4 What is the name of a big city in your country?
5 Are you near that city now?
6 Are you in that city now?

Vocabulary

3 Look.

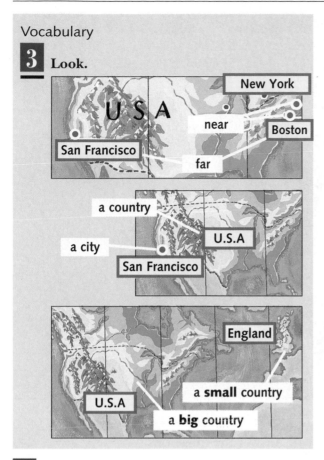

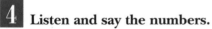

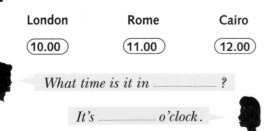

4 Listen and say the numbers.

10	11	12	13
ten	*eleven*	*twelve*	*thirteen*

14	15	16	17
fourteen	*fifteen*	*sixteen*	*seventeen*

18	19	20
eighteen	*nineteen*	*twenty*

5 Ask and answer the questions.

London	Rome	Cairo
(10.00)	(11.00)	(12.00)

What time is it in .... ?

It's .... o'clock.

Grammar

6 Look.

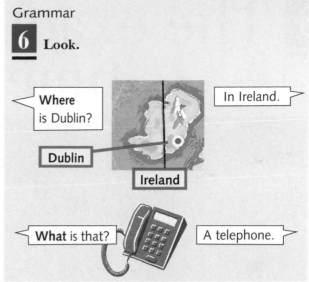

Where is Dublin?

In Ireland.

Dublin

Ireland

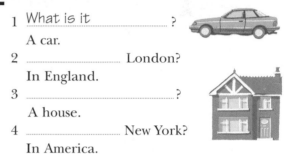

What is that?

A telephone.

7 Write 'what is it?' or 'where is...?'

1 <u>What is it</u> .... ?
  A car.
2 .... London?
  In England.
3 .... ?
  A house.
4 .... New York?
  In America.

8 Answer the questions.

1 Where is Cork?
2 Where is Glasgow?
3 Where is Manchester?
4 What is the name of a city in your country?
5 Is it a big city or a small city?

Pronunciation

9 Listen and say the words.

1 big, six, England, city
2 city, three, country
3 London, country, number
4 small, four
5 no, telephone, Toronto, Glasgow

Classic Extra page 94

3 The exact time

This is the Green Parrot. It is a small café in London. It isn't far from Victoria Station.

The man in the picture is Larry Jasper. The woman is Diana Brentano.

DIANA   Excuse me. What time is it, please?

LARRY   The time?

DIANA   Yes. What time is it?

LARRY   Six... er... six fourteen.

DIANA   Six fourteen?

LARRY   Yes... No! That's wrong.

DIANA   Pardon?

LARRY   It's six fifteen now.

DIANA   Six fifteen? Quarter past six?

LARRY   Yes. Six fifteen and... er... ten seconds.
That's the exact time.

DIANA   Thank you.

1 Answer the questions.

1 Is the Green Parrot a man?
2 Is the Green Parrot a woman?
3 Is it a city?
4 Is it a country?
5 What is it?
6 Where is it?

2 What about you?

1 Where are you?
2 Are you near a café?
3 Are you near a school?
4 Are you in a school?
5 What is the exact time?

3 Listen and answer the question.
What is the exact time in...?

1 London   4 Tokyo
2 Berlin   5 Bangkok
3 Moscow   6 Toronto

Vocabulary

4 Look.

The exact time

second

hour   12   minute

2 + 2 = 5   ✗   wrong

2 + 2 = 4   ✓   right

Colours

black	white	red	green	blue	brown

5 Listen and say the words.

24 hours   *A day.*   28–31 days   *A month.*

seven days   *A week.*   12 months   *A year.*

6 Listen and say the numbers.

21	30	32
twenty-one	*thirty*	*thirty-two*
40	43	50
forty	*forty-three*	*fifty*
54	60	65
fifty-four	*sixty*	*sixty-five*

7 Listen and read. What time is it?

Six fifteen.
or
Quarter past six.

Six thirty.
or
Half past six.

Six forty-five.
or
Quarter to seven.

8 Ask and answer the questions.

What time is it in .... ?

It's ....

LONDON	6.15	ATHENS	9.15
PARIS	7.15	SHANGHAI	1.15
HOLLYWOOD	10.15	TOKYO	2.15

Pronunciation

9 Listen and say the words.

1 r<u>igh</u>t, wh<u>i</u>te
2 <u>r</u>ight, <u>wr</u>ong
3 b<u>lue</u>, <u>you</u>, n<u>ew</u>
4 <u>th</u>anks, <u>th</u>ir<u>t</u>een, <u>th</u>ree
5 <u>i</u>t, min<u>u</u>te
6 n<u>ow</u>, h<u>our</u>

Classic Extra page 95

4

Where are you from?

A man and a woman are in a café in London.

LARRY	Where are you from?
DIANA	Australia.
LARRY	Where in Australia?
DIANA	Pardon?
LARRY	Australia is a big country. Where in Australia are you from?
DIANA	Manley.
LARRY	Manley? Where's that?
DIANA	It's near Sydney. What about you? Where are you from?
LARRY	I'm from Liverpool.

1 Answer the questions.

1 Where is Diana now?
2 Is she from London?
3 Where is she from?
4 Where is Larry from?
5 Is he in Liverpool now?

2 What about you?

1 What country are you from?
2 Is it a big country?
3 Are you from a big city?
4 Are you in a big city?

Grammar

3 Look.

We write:

I	am
He	
She	is
It	
You	
We	are
They	

We say:

I'm
He's
She's
It's
You're
We're
They're

---

4 Answer the questions.

1 Is Larry from London?

No, ... from ....

2 Is Diana from London?

No, ... Manley, near Sydney.

3 Is London in Australia?

No, ...

4 Where are Larry and Diana now?

....

5 What about you? Are you from London?

No, ...

6 Where are you now?

....

Vocabulary

6 Listen and say the names of the countries.

1 France
2 Spain
3 Italy
4 Germany
5 Brazil
6 Japan
7 Poland

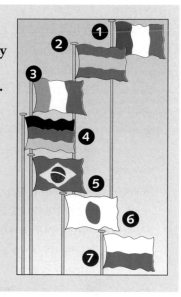

Pronunciation

5 Listen and say the words.

1 London, colour, number, country
2 Spain, say, they, Australia
3 England, Italy, six, city
4 Poland, woman, Germany, Brazil

---

7 Ask and answer the questions.

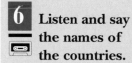

Where's Rio?   *In Brazil.*

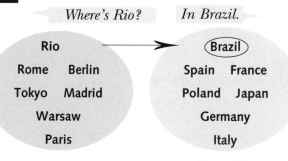

Rio
Rome   Berlin
Tokyo   Madrid
Warsaw
Paris

Brazil
Spain   France
Poland   Japan
Germany
Italy

Classic Extra page 95

5 How much is it?

 The man in this picture is a waiter. The woman is Susan Farr.

SUSAN	What's that?
WAITER	This? A sandwich.
SUSAN	Yes. But what kind of sandwich? What's in it?
WAITER	Cheese.
SUSAN	What kind of cheese?
WAITER	Swiss cheese. Cheese from Switzerland.
SUSAN	How much is it?
WAITER	One pound seventy-five.
SUSAN	All right. A Swiss cheese sandwich, please.
WAITER	Is that all?
SUSAN	No. And a cup of coffee, too. How much is that?
WAITER	Two pounds sixty.
SUSAN	Pardon? Two pounds sixty for a cup of coffee?
WAITER	No. One pound seventy-five for a Swiss cheese sandwich and eighty-five pence for a cup of coffee.

1 Answer the questions.

1 What is in the sandwich?
2 What is Swiss cheese?
3 How much is the sandwich?
4 How much is the cup of coffee?

2 What about you?

1 Are you from Switzerland?
2 How much is a cup of coffee in your country?
3 How much is a cheese sandwich in your country?

3 Listen and say the numbers.

70	*seventy*	77	*seventy-seven*
80	*eighty*	88	*eighty-eight*
90	*ninety*	99	*ninety-nine*
100	*one hundred*	101	*one hundred and one*
200	*two hundred*	202	*two hundred and two*

4 Say the numbers.

22	*twenty-two*	76	....
33	*thirty-three*	86	....
55	....	103	....
95	....	212	....

Vocabulary

5 Look.

1 a bottle	**4** a bottle of wine
2 a cup	**5** a mug of coffee
3 a glass	**6** a glass of water
	7 cheese

6 What is it?

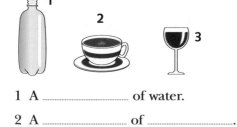

1 A _____ of water.

2 A _____ of _____ .

3 _____ glass _____ _____ .

7 Listen. How much is it?

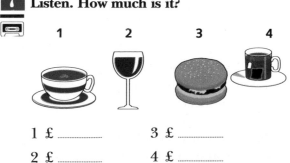

| 1 | 2 | 3 | 4 |

1 £ _____   3 £ _____

2 £ _____   4 £ _____

Grammar

8 Look. 'A', 'this' or 'that'?

a man   this man   that man

9 Write 'a', 'this', 'that' and 'cup' or 'bottle'.

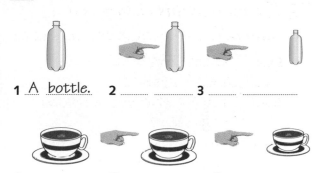

1 A bottle.   2 _____ _____   3 _____ _____

4 _____ _____   5 _____ _____   6 _____ _____

10 Listen and say the words.

Italian, Polish, German, Spanish, French, Japanese

11 Where are they from? Ask and answer the questions.

Roman is from Warsaw.
Vera is from Berlin.
Claudia is from Rome.
Pilar is from Madrid.
Pierre is from Paris.
Osamu is from Tokyo.

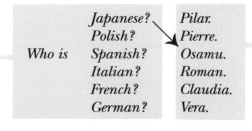

	Japanese?	Pilar.
	Polish?	Pierre.
Who is	Spanish?	Osamu.
	Italian?	Roman.
	French?	Claudia.
	German?	Vera.

Classic Extra page 96

A street near Victoria

6

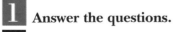
This is a street in London. It is very near Victoria Station. There are a lot of shops and pubs near Victoria Station. There are a lot of hotels and restaurants, too.
It is six fifteen in the evening. There are a lot of people in the street and in the shops, pubs and restaurants near Victoria.
A man is in a shop near Victoria Station.

BERNARD	How much is this magazine?
WOMAN	The price is there.
BERNARD	Where?
WOMAN	There. Look. Two pounds.
BERNARD	Oh, yes.

1 Answer the questions.

1 Who is that man ?
2 Is he in a pub?
3 Is he in a restaurant?
4 Where is he?
5 How much is that magazine?

2 What about you?

1 Are you near a station now?
2 Are you in a hotel?
3 Are you in a school?
4 What time is it where you are?
5 Is it morning, afternoon or evening?
6 Are you near a restaurant?
7 Are you near people?
8 Are you near a lot of people now?

Vocabulary

3 Look.

7 a.m.	3 p.m.
morning	afternoon
6 p.m.	11 p.m.
evening	night

a newspaper   a magazine   a book

people   books

a lot of people   a lot of books

How **much** is the book?

The **price** of this book is six ninety-five.

£6.95

The book **costs** six ninety-five.

4 What is the wrong word?

1 book (man) newspaper magazine
2 cup sandwich bottle glass
3 coffee tea cheese water
4 Italy Spain France German
5 Germany Spanish French Italian
6 second minute hour shop
7 minute sandwich hour second
8 day number week month

Grammar

5 Listen and say the words.

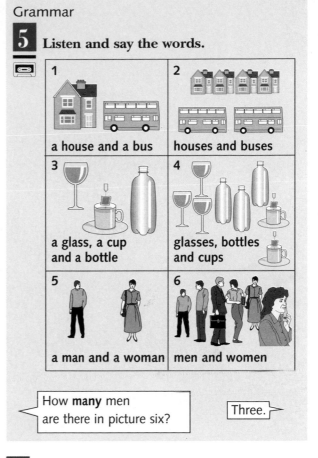

1	2
a house and a bus	houses and buses
3	4
a glass, a cup and a bottle	glasses, bottles and cups
5	6
a man and a woman	men and women

How **many** men are there in picture six?

Three.

6 Answer the questions.

1 How many women are there in picture six?
2 Now look at picture five. Are there three women there, too?
3 How many women are there in picture five?
4 How many glasses are there in picture four?
5 How many houses are there in picture two?

Pronunciation

7 Listen and say the words.

1 <u>s</u>even, <u>c</u>ity, hou<u>se</u>, bu<u>s</u>, gla<u>ss</u>
2 book<u>s</u>, shop<u>s</u>, cup<u>s</u>, minute<u>s</u>, street<u>s</u>
3 <u>z</u>ero, maga<u>z</u>ine, i<u>s</u>, hi<u>s</u>, chee<u>se</u>
4 maga<u>z</u>ine<u>s</u>, pub<u>s</u>, second<u>s</u>, hou<u>se</u>s
5 i<u>s</u>, bu<u>se</u>s, glas<u>se</u>s, hou<u>se</u>s

Classic Extra page 96

7 London

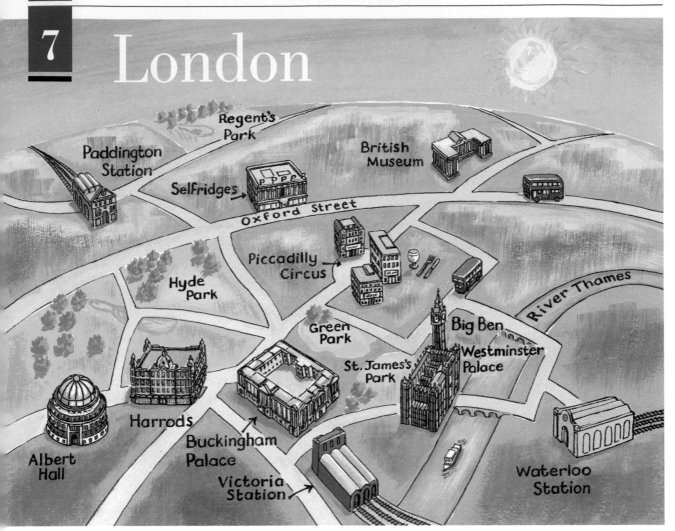

Paddington Station
Regent's Park
British Museum
Selfridges
Oxford Street
Piccadilly Circus
Hyde Park
Green Park
Big Ben
River Thames
St. James's Park
Westminster Palace
Harrods
Albert Hall
Buckingham Palace
Victoria Station
Waterloo Station

London is a very big city. Seven million people live there.

There are four big parks in the centre of London. That's Hyde Park on the left. It's near Oxford Street. Selfridges is in Oxford Street. It's a big department store. Harrods is a big department store, too, but it isn't in Oxford Street. There are a lot of department stores in London.

Victoria Station is near Buckingham Palace. The Queen lives there. Larry Jasper lives near Victoria Station, too. Waterloo and Paddington are stations, too. Paddington is on the left and Waterloo is on the right. The weather is good today.

1 Right or wrong?

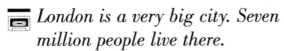

| London is small. | That's **wrong**. |
| London is big. | That's **right**. |

1 Hyde Park is a big park in the centre of London.
2 Selfridges is in Oxford Street but it isn't near Waterloo.
3 Paddington is a big department store, too.
4 There is one big station in London.
5 The Queen lives in Victoria Station.
6 She lives near Victoria Station.
7 Waterloo is the station on the right and Paddington is the station on the left.
8 Victoria is on the right, too.

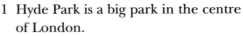

Vocabulary

2 Look.

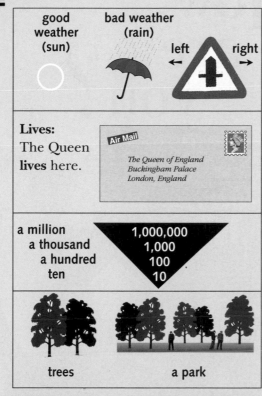

good weather (sun)	bad weather (rain)		
○		left ← ↑ → right	

Lives:
The Queen **lives** here.

Air Mail

The Queen of England
Buckingham Palace
London, England

a million	1,000,000
a thousand	1,000
a hundred	100
ten	10

trees   a park

a department store

3 What about you?

1 What is the name of a big city in your country?
2 How many people live in that city?
3 Are you there now?
4 Is there a big department store in that city?
5 Are there parks, restaurants and shops there?
6 Are there a lot of good restaurants there?

Grammar

4 Look.

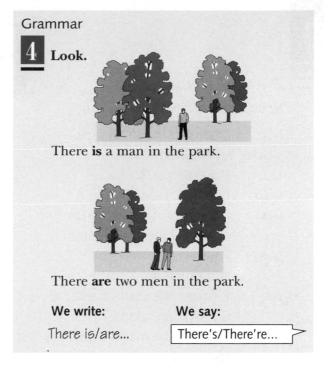

There **is** a man in the park.

There **are** two men in the park.

We write:	**We say:**
There is/are...	There's/There're...

5 Look at the picture on page 18. Write 'is' or 'are'.

1 There __is__ a big park near Piccadilly.
2 There _____ two big department stores in this city.
3 There _____ a good restaurant near Piccadilly, too.
4 There _____ a lot of houses and shops in this city.
5 There _____ a museum near Regent's Park.
6 There _____ two parks near Victoria Station.
7 There _____ four big parks in London.

6 Look.

13	thirteen	30	thirty
14	fourteen	40	forty

🔲 Now listen. Circle the right number.

1	(13) 30	4	16 60
2	14 40	5	17 70
3	15 50	6	19 90

Classic Extra page 97

8

How are you?

A woman and a man are in an office in London.

JACK	Good afternoon, Shirley.
SHIRLEY	Hello, Jack.
JACK	How are you?
SHIRLEY	I'm tired. How are you?
JACK	Fine, thanks. Who are the two people in the photograph?
SHIRLEY	Their names are Jasper and Brentano.
JACK	Is Jasper the man's name? Or is it the woman's name?
SHIRLEY	Jasper is the man's name. His first name is Larry. The woman's first name is Diana.
JACK	Diana Brentano? Is she Italian?
SHIRLEY	No. She's Australian.
JACK	What about the man? Where's he from?
SHIRLEY	Liverpool, but he lives in London now. Look. This is his address.

1 Answer the questions.

1 Who are the people in the office?
2 Is he tired?
3 Is she tired?
4 Who is the man in the photograph?
5 What is his first name?
6 What is his last name?
7 Who is the woman in the photograph?
8 Is Diana her first name or her last name?

2 What about you?

1 How are you today?
2 Are you tired?
3 What's your first name?
4 What's your last name?

3 Listen.
Then answer the questions.

1 What is his first name?
2 Where is he from?
3 Where does he live?

Vocabulary

 Look.

Hello. Hello. Goodbye.

7 a.m. — Good morning.

3 p.m. — Good afternoon.

6 p.m. — Good evening.

11 p.m. — Good night.

How are you?
Very well.

Fine, thanks. How are you?

I'm tired.

The woman's name is Diana Brentano.

The man's name is Larry Jasper.

5 What about you?

1 What is your first name?
2 Is that a man's name or a woman's name?
3 Is there a man near you?
4 What is his name?
5 Is there a woman near you?
6 What is her name?
7 Are there people near you?
8 What are their names?

Grammar

6 **Look.**

Manchester   London

Who is he? — Bernard.
Where is he? — In London.
Where is he from? — Manchester.

7 Answer the questions.

1 Who is the man? _Larry Jasper._
2 Who is the woman? ....
3 Where is she from? ....
4 Where is he from? ....
5 Where are they now? ....

Pronunciation

8 **Listen and say the words.**

1 six, is, Italian, English
2 three, she, tea, people
3 you, new
4 tired, five, my, nine

Classic Extra page 97

9 Is that your wallet?

📼 *Susan Farr is from Canada. She is in London.*

SUSAN	Is this the bus to Paddington?
MAN	The thirty-six.
SUSAN	Pardon?
MAN	The bus to Paddington is the thirty-six.
SUSAN	The thirty-six?
MAN	Yes. The number thirty-six. Look. There's a thirty-six there.
SUSAN	Where?
MAN	Behind this bus. Can you see it?

1 Answer these questions.

1 Is that the bus to Paddington Station?
2 What number is the bus to Paddington Station?
3 Where is the thirty-six?

📼 *Susan is on the thirty-six bus now. The man's name is Bernard.*

SUSAN	Excuse me. Is that your wallet?
BERNARD	My wallet? Where?
SUSAN	There. It's on the seat, next to you.
BERNARD	Yes... yes, that's my wallet. Thank you. Thank you very much!

2 Now answer these questions.

1 Where is Susan now?
2 What is the man's name?
3 Is that her wallet?
4 Where is it?

3 What about you?

1 Is your teacher near you?
2 Is he or she next to you?
3 Is he or she behind you?
4 Where is your teacher now?

Vocabulary

4 Look.

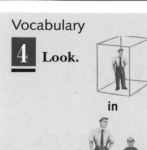

in   on   to   from

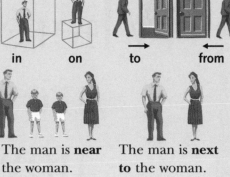

The man is **near** the woman.

The man is **next to** the woman.

The thirty-six bus is **behind** the ninety-two bus.

The seventy-three bus is **in front of** the ninety-two bus.

5 Answer the questions.

1 Who is behind Larry and Diana?
2 Who is in front of Shirley?
3 Who is next to Larry?

Grammar

6 Look.

What is **her** name?

What is **his** name?

What are **their** names?

7 Write the answers with 'her', 'your', 'their', 'his', or 'my'.

1 What are ___their___ names?
  Larry and Diana.

2 What is _____ name?
  Diana.

3 What is _____ name?
  Larry.

4 "Hello, _____ name's Susan."

5 "What's _____ name?"
  "My name's Bernard."

6 "Is _____ name Bernard?"
  "No, my name's Larry."

7 _____ name is Shirley.
  She is behind Diana.

Pronunciation

8 Listen and say the words.

1 <u>sh</u>e, <u>sh</u>op, sta<u>ti</u>on
2 re<u>st</u>aurant, <u>str</u>eet, <u>st</u>ation
3 b<u>u</u>s, fr<u>o</u>nt, c<u>ou</u>ntry
4 maga<u>z</u>ine, buse<u>s</u>, house<u>s</u>

10

Where are we now?

A man and a woman are on a bus in London.

SUSAN	Excuse me. Where are we now?
BERNARD	Hyde Park.
SUSAN	Are we near Paddington?
BERNARD	It isn't very far.
SUSAN	How many stops is it from here?
BERNARD	Well... Marble Arch is the next stop.
SUSAN	Pardon? What's the next stop?
BERNARD	Marble Arch. It's near Oxford Street. Look. That's Marble Arch. There. Can you see it?
SUSAN	Oh, yes. How many stops is Paddington from Marble Arch?
BERNARD	Two, I think. No. Three.
SUSAN	So, Paddington is the second or third stop after Marble Arch? Is that right?
BERNARD	Yes.

1 **Right or wrong?**

1 Susan and Bernard aren't very near Hyde Park.
2 They're very near Hyde Park.
3 They're near Oxford Street, too.
4 Paddington is very far from Oxford Street.
5 Paddington is the next stop.
6 The next stop is near Oxford Street.

2 **Listen and say the numbers.**

fifth
fourth
third
second
first

Vocabulary

3 **Look.**

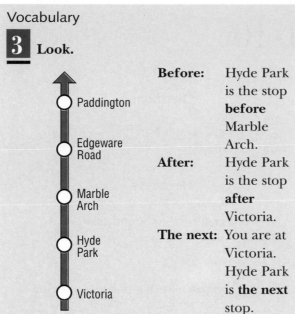

Before: Hyde Park is the stop **before** Marble Arch.

After: Hyde Park is the stop **after** Victoria.

The next: You are at Victoria. Hyde Park is **the next** stop.

4 **Answer the questions.**

1 What is the stop after Edgeware Road?
2 What is the stop before Edgeware Road?
3 You are at Victoria now. What is the next stop?
4 Is Paddington the second stop after Hyde Park? Or is it the third stop?
5 Can A see B?
6 Can B see A?

 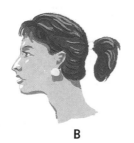

A   B

Pronunciation

5 **Listen and say the words.**

1 f<u>ar</u>, c<u>ar</u>, <u>are</u>
2 cl<u>o</u>ck, wh<u>a</u>t
3 ne<u>x</u>t, <u>s</u>tation, <u>s</u>top
4 ne<u>x</u>t, Vi<u>c</u>toria, park, e<u>x</u>cuse
5 <u>th</u>ree, <u>th</u>irty, <u>th</u>irteen

Grammar

6 **Look.**

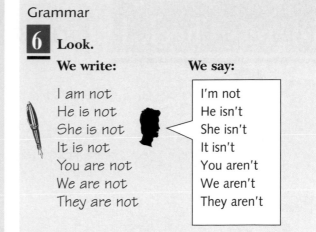

We write:	We say:
I am not	I'm not
He is not	He isn't
She is not	She isn't
It is not	It isn't
You are not	You aren't
We are not	We aren't
They are not	They aren't

7 **Write 'is', 'isn't', 'are', or 'aren't'.**

1 Larry __is__ from Liverpool but he _____ in Liverpool now.
2 Diana _____ from Australia but she _____ there now.
3 Larry and Diana _____ in Liverpool and they _____ in Australia.
4 They _____ in London.

8 **What about you? Write and say sentences.**

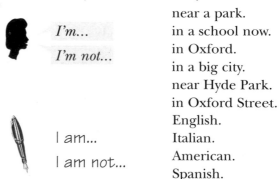

I'm...
I'm not...

I am...
I am not...

near a park.
in a school now.
in Oxford.
in a big city.
near Hyde Park.
in Oxford Street.
English.
Italian.
American.
Spanish.
from a big city.

Classic Extra page 98

Progress Check 1 Units 1-10

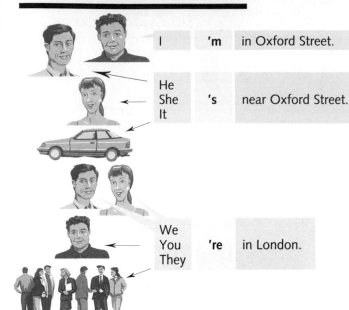

I	'm	in Oxford Street.
He She It	's	near Oxford Street.
We You They	're	in London.

Questions

Am Is Are	I the car they	in London? near Oxford Street?

Negatives

I They The car	'm not aren't isn't	in Manchester.

There **is**	a park near the station. It is called Green Park.
There **are**	two stations near the river.

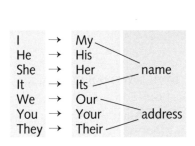

I	→	My
He	→	His
She	→	Her
It	→	Its
We	→	Our
You	→	Your
They	→	Their

name

address

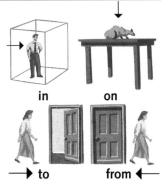

in   on

→ to   from ←

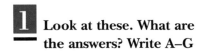

Numbers: one, two, three; ten, twenty, thirty; a hundred, a thousand, a million.
First, second, third, fourth, fifth.
Colours: white, black, red, green, blue, brown.
Countries: France/French, Germany/German, Poland/Polish etc.

Now test yourself!

1 Look at these. What are the answers? Write A–G

1 Good morning.
2 How are you?
3 What's that?
4 Who is that?
5 Where is she from?
6 What kind of coffee is that?
7 How much is it?

C	A A photograph.
☐	B Canada.
☐	C Good morning.
☐	D Brazilian. It's very good.
☐	E Susan Farr.
☐	F £6.99.
☐	G Fine, thanks. What about you?

2 Write 'is' or 'are'.

1 Larry is from Liverpool. _Is_

Bernard from Liverpool, too?

2 New York and Toronto are big cities.

_____ London and Dublin big cities, too?

3 Paddington is a station.

_____ Victoria a station, too?

4 I'm tired. What about you?

_____ you tired, too?

5 Bernard and Larry are English.

_____ Susan and Diana English, too?

3 Write 'isn't', 'aren't' or ''m not'.

1 Liverpool is near Manchester, but

Oxford _isn't_ near Manchester. It's

near London.

2 Oxford is near London, but

Liverpool _____ near London. It's

near Manchester.

3 New York and Chicago are in America.

Liverpool and Manchester _____

in America.

4 You're tired but I'_____ tired.

5 You and Larry are tired but we

_____ tired.

4 Write 'your', 'my', 'her', 'their' or 'our'.

1 I live in London. _My_ address is 19

Green Park Street.

2 Diana lives in London, too. _____

address is 57 Rutland Street.

3 What about Bernard and Susan? What

are _____ addresses?

4 We live in Manchester. _____ address

is 25 Stockton Avenue.

5 What about you? _____ address isn't

here. What is it?

5 What is the next word?

1 One book, two _books._

2 One man, two _____

3 One woman, two _____

4 One glass, two _____

5 One house, two _____

6 One shop, a lot of _____

6 Write 'there' or 'it'.

1 London is a city. _It_ is

in England.

2 London is a big city. _____ are a lot of

parks there.

3 _____ are three big department stores in

Oxford Street.

4 Paddington is a station. _____ isn't far

from Oxford Street.

5 _____ is a big station near Buckingham

Palace, too.

6 _____ are a lot of shops, pubs, hotels

and restaurants near Buckingham Palace.

7 The weather isn't good today. _____ is

very bad.

7 What is the name of the country?

1 Larry is English.

He is from _England._

2 Diana is Australian. She _____ from

_____

3 Yoshiko is Japanese. She _____

_____ _____

4 Heinz is German. He _____

_____

5 Maria is Italian. She _____ _____

_____

6 Pilar is Spanish. She _____ _____

_____

11 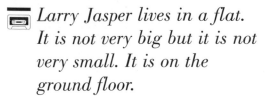 Where do they live?

Larry Jasper lives in a flat. It is not very big but it is not very small. It is on the ground floor.

His address is one hundred and seventy-two Green Parrot Street, London. Bernard Winter lives in a small house near a school. His address is fifteen Merton Street, Oxford. Oxford is a city near London.

1 Right or wrong?

1 Larry lives in a big house.
2 He lives in a flat but it isn't very big.
3 He lives on the ground floor.
4 Bernard lives near a school.
5 Bernard lives in a city near London.

Larry and a woman are in a café in London.

LARRY	Where do you live, Diana?
DIANA	Here. In London.
LARRY	Yes, but where in London?
DIANA	In Rutland Street.
LARRY	Rutland Street? Where's that?
DIANA	Near Paddington Station.

2 Yes or no?

Is Larry in his flat now? No.
Is he in a café? Yes.

1 Is Rutland Street in London?
2 Does Diana live in Oxford?
3 Docs she live in London?
4 Does she live near Paddington Station?

3 Listen to Susan Farr.

1 Where is she from?
2 Where does she live now?
3 What is her address?

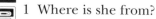

Vocabulary

4 Look.

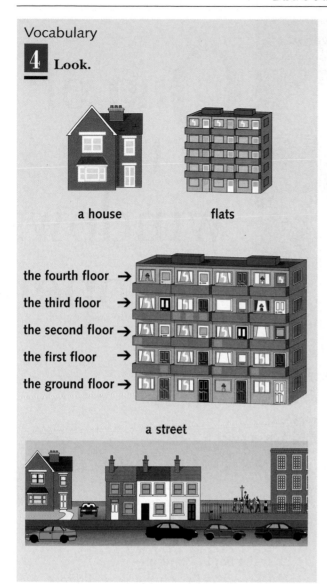

a house   flats

the fourth floor →
the third floor →
the second floor →
the first floor →
the ground floor →

a street

5 Say a word on the left. Then say the opposite.

first	*small*
white	*bad*
here	*far*
left	*last*
good	*right*
near	*there*
big	*black*
right	*wrong*

Grammar

6 Look.

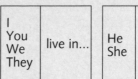

I You We They	live in...	He She	lives in...

7 Say the right sentences.

1 Bernard lives in a flat.
   That's wrong. He lives in a house.

2 Larry lives in Oxford.
3 He lives in a house.
4 Larry and Diana live in Oxford.
5 You live in a school.
6 You live in a very big flat in New York.

8 Write about Bernard, Larry and Diana.

1 Bernard __lives__ in Oxford.
2 _____ in a house.
3 Larry _____ in a flat in London.
4 Larry and Bernard _____ in England.
5 Larry and Diana _____ in London.

9 What about you? Write and say sentences.

I live	in near	a a big a small	flat. city. park.

I live in...
        near...

Pronunciation

10 Listen and say the words.

1 si̱x, li̱ve, li̱ves
2 fi̱ve, whi̱te, ri̱ght
3 go̱od, wo̱man
4 fo̱ur, do̱or, flo̱or
5 li̱ve, li̱ves, wo̱men
6 maga̱zine, live̱s

Classic Extra page 99

12

One of the windows is open

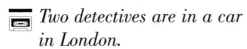

Two detectives are in a car in London.

SHIRLEY　Larry lives in a flat in that building.

JACK　Which flat?

SHIRLEY　The flat on the ground floor. And look. He isn't there now. The lights in his flat are off.

JACK　Yes, I can see that.

SHIRLEY　And look at that.

JACK　What?

SHIRLEY　One of the windows is open. Can you see it?

JACK　No, I can't. Which window is open?

SHIRLEY　The window on the left, next to the door.

JACK　Oh, yes. I can see it now. You're right. One of the windows isn't closed. Good. Very good!

1 **Yes or no?**

Does Larry live in a house? No.

Does he live in a flat? Yes.

1　Does Larry live in a flat?
2　Is the flat in London?
3　Does Larry live on the second floor?
4　Does he live on the ground floor?
5　Is he in the flat now?
6　Are the two detectives in Larry's flat?
7　Can they see the flat?
8　Are the lights off?
9　Are all the windows in his flat closed?

2 **What about you?**

1　Do you live in a flat?
2　Do you live in a house?
3　Is it very big?
4　Is it very small?
5　Do you live in a big city?
6　Do you live in a big country?
7　What's your address?

Vocabulary

3 Look.

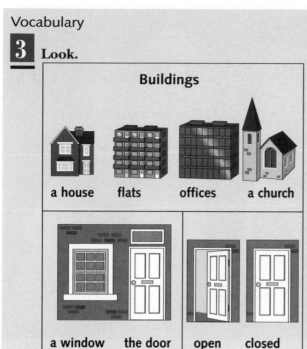

Buildings

a house   flats   offices   a church

a window   the door   open   closed

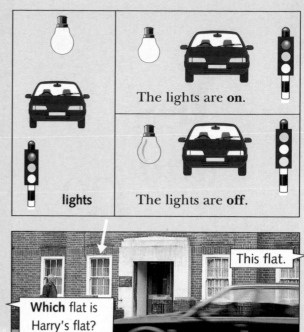

The lights are **on**.

lights   The lights are **off**.

Which flat is Harry's flat?

This flat.

Pronunciation

4 **Listen and say the words.**

1 h<u>ou</u>se, h<u>ow</u>, n<u>ow</u>
2 h<u>er</u>, ch<u>ur</u>ch
3 n<u>o</u>, cl<u>o</u>sed, <u>o</u>pen, wind<u>ow</u>
4 r<u>igh</u>t, l<u>igh</u>t, n<u>igh</u>t, wh<u>i</u>te
5 b<u>ui</u>lding, M<u>i</u>lan, m<u>i</u>llion
6 <u>ch</u>ur<u>ch</u>, whi<u>ch</u>, ar<u>ch</u>

Grammar

5 Look.

Can you **see** the numbers?   **123**   Yes, I **can**.

Can you **see** the numbers now?   123   No, I **can't**.

I You He She We They	can can't	see	the numbers. the lights. the people. the photograph. the sun. the address.

6 **What can you see in the picture? Ask and answer the questions.**

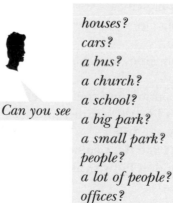

Can you see

houses?
cars?
a bus?
a church?
a school?
a big park?
a small park?
people?
a lot of people?
offices?

Yes, I can.

No, I can't.

Classic Extra page 99

31

13

Yes *and* no

Larry Jasper and Diana Brentano
are in a café in London. Diana is
from Australia. Larry is English.

LARRY	Do you like England?
DIANA	Yes and no.
LARRY	Yes and no? What does that mean?
DIANA	It means there are things I like. And there are things I don't like.
LARRY	Oh? What are the things you like?
DIANA	I like London. It's a nice city and I like big cities.
LARRY	And what are the things you don't like?
DIANA	I don't like the weather here. And I don't like the food. I think it's terrible.
LARRY	Is that all?
DIANA	No. I don't like the men. I don't like the men here at all!

1 Right or wrong?

1 Diana likes big cities.
2 She likes big cities but she doesn't like London.
3 She likes big cities and she likes London, too.
4 She likes London and the weather there.
5 She doesn't like the weather and she doesn't like the food.
6 She doesn't like the weather and the food in London but she likes the men there.

2 What about you?

1 What are two things you like?
2 What are two things you don't like?
3 Do you like big cities?
4 What kind of food do you like?
5 Is the weather good today?

3 Listen to Susan. Answer the questions.

1 Does Susan like London?
2 Does she like big cities?
3 What does she like in England?
4 What doesn't she like?

Grammar

4 Look.

I like it. I don't like it.

Vocabulary

5 Look.

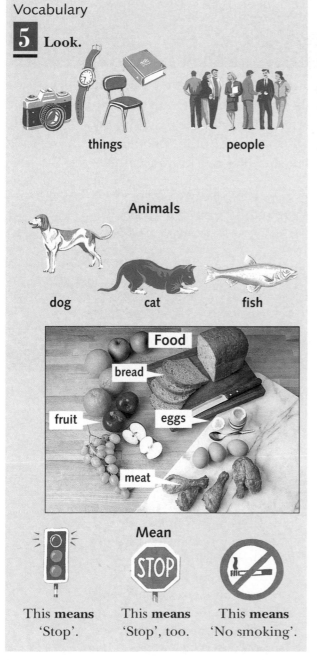

things   people

Animals

dog   cat   fish

Food

bread
fruit   eggs
meat

Mean

This **means** 'Stop'.   This **means** 'Stop', too.   This **means** 'No smoking'.

Pronunciation

6 Listen and say the words.

1 three, thirteen, thirty, things
2 this, that, there, the
3 she, he, cheese, people, mean
4 two, food, school, too, fruit, do
5 seven, red, bread

7 Talk about Diana.

*She **likes** cats, but she **doesn't like** dogs.*

*She **likes**... music, but she **doesn't like**... music.*

Here are things Diana **likes**.

cats	rock music
Italian food	coffee
fish	the sun

And here are things Diana **doesn't like**.

dogs	classical music
English food	tea
meat	rain

8 What about you? Talk and write.

1 What are three things you like?
   I like

2 What are three things you don't like?
   I don't like

I like... but I don't like...

Classic Extra page 100

14 Four people

Bernard Winter lives and works in Oxford. He works in a museum there. He buys pictures. Bernard is an art expert. He is very interested in modern art.

Susan Farr lives in New York. She works there, too. She is a journalist. She writes articles for a magazine. She works in a small office. A lot of other people work there, too, but she likes her job very much.

Larry Jasper lives in London. He buys and sells cars. Some are old and some are new. He's very interested in money, too. He thinks about money all the time.

Diana Brentano is a make-up artist. She works in television.

1 Answer the questions.

1 Where does Bernard live?
2 Where does he work?
3 What is Larry interested in?
4 Where does Susan live?
5 Where does she work?
6 Does she like her job?

2 What about you?

1 Do you work in an office?
2 Do you work in a museum?
3 Do you sell things?
4 Do you buy things?
5 Are you interested in money?
6 Are you interested in art, too?
7 What is one other thing you are interested in?

Vocabulary

3 Look.

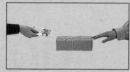 

buy   sell   old   new

1 **Other:** Susan is in this photograph. Four **other** people are in the photograph, too.
2 **Work:** Susan **works** in an office. The other people in the photograph **work** in the same office.
3 **Some** means 'not all'. **Some** of the people in the photograph are men. **Some** are women. **Some** men like football. **Some** men don't like it.

£ $ DM   ¥

4 **Interested:** Larry is very **interested** in money
5 **Think:** He **thinks** about money all the time.

Pronunciation

4 Listen and say the words.

1 <u>th</u>ree, <u>th</u>ink, <u>th</u>ing
2 <u>th</u>is, <u>th</u>at, <u>th</u>e
3 b<u>uy</u>, m<u>y</u>, <u>I</u>, f<u>i</u>ve
4 l<u>i</u>ve, <u>E</u>ngland, <u>I</u>taly, s<u>i</u>x
5 <u>s</u>econd<u>s</u>, <u>s</u>ell, work<u>s</u>, think<u>s</u>
6 <u>z</u>oo, i<u>s</u>, hi<u>s</u>, thing<u>s</u>, buy<u>s</u>, sell<u>s</u>, mu<u>s</u>eum

Grammar

5 Look.

I	live
You	work
We	think
You	like
They	know

He	live**s**
She	work**s**
It	think**s**
	know**s**
	like**s**

6 Write the sentences.

Pat   Olga   Martin   Booker

1 Olga <u>works</u> in an office.
2 Pat _____ in the same office.
3 Olga and Pat _____ in the same office.
4 Booker and Martin _____ in the office, too.
5 Martin _____ his job very much.
6 Olga, Pat and Booker _____ their jobs, too.

7 Ask other people questions.

Where do you live/work?

Are you interested in   golf?
                    football?
                    art?

8 Talk and write about yourself.

My name is...

I'm interested in...

I work in...
I live in...

Classic Extra page 100

15

What do you do?

A man and a woman are in a café in London.

LARRY	What do you do, Diana?
DIANA	I'm a make-up artist.
LARRY	What's a make-up artist?
DIANA	You don't know?
LARRY	No. I don't know. What does a make-up artist do?
DIANA	A make-up artist puts make-up on people's faces.
LARRY	Oh. I understand now. Do you work in films?
DIANA	No. I work in television. What do you do?
LARRY	I buy and sell cars.
DIANA	What kind of cars do you sell?
LARRY	Some are old and some are new. But they're all expensive. They're classic cars. Very rich people buy them.
DIANA	Are you very rich, too?
LARRY	I'm not very poor.

1 **Answer the questions.**

1 What does a make-up artist do?
2 What does Larry do?
3 What kind of cars does he sell?
4 What kind of people does he sell the cars to?

2 **What about you?**

1 What do you do?
2 Are you very rich?
3 Are you interested in expensive cars?
4 What are you interested in?

3 **A man and a woman talk. Listen and answer the questions.**

1 What is the man's name?
2 What is the woman's name?
3 Where is he?
4 Where is she?

Vocabulary

 4. Look.

1 "What do you do?" means 'What is your job?'

2 **Know:** You **know** the words sandwich, pizza, good and bad. You know what the words mean.

3 **Understand:** "I **understand**" means 'I know what the words mean'. "I **don't understand**" means 'I don't know what the words mean'.

4 **Rich** people are people with a lot of money. The opposite of rich is **poor.**

5 One of the cars is very **expensive**. **Expensive** things cost a lot of money. The opposite of expensive is **cheap**.

 5 Look at the pictures. Answer the questions.

1 Which car do you think is very expensive? The big car? Or the small car?

2 Here are three words. The first is Spanish, the second is Italian and the third is German. Do you understand them?
'Coche', 'macchina', 'Auto'.

3 What does the German word 'Auto' mean? Do you know?

4 Do you know the English words for 'coche', 'macchina' and 'Auto'? Say them.

Pronunciation

 6 Listen and say the words.

1 <u>u</u>nderstand, c<u>ou</u>ntry, m<u>o</u>ney
2 ch<u>ea</u>p, p<u>eo</u>ple, s<u>ee</u>
3 h<u>er</u>, w<u>or</u>d, w<u>or</u>ld, w<u>or</u>k
4 m<u>ore</u>, d<u>oor</u>, <u>or</u>, f<u>our</u>,

Grammar

 7 Look at the questions.

He She	lives likes	in London. white wine.
Does **Does**	he she	**live** **like**	in London? white wine?

8 Write questions.

1 Bernard lives in Oxford.
Does Bernard _live_ in Oxford?

2 'Wonderful' means 'very good'.
.... 'terrible' .... 'very bad'?

3 Diana likes Italian food.
.... Diana .... Italian food?

4 Larry sells expensive cars.
.... Larry .... expensive cars?

5 Bernard understands French.
.... Bernard .... French?

Grammar

 9 Look.

I You They	**like** **live** **work**	Spanish food. in a big city. in a shop.
Do	we you they	**like** **live** **work**	Spanish food? in a big city? in a shop?

10 Write questions.

1 You understand all the words.
_Do_ you _understand_ all the words?

2 You like expensive things.
.... you .... expensive things?

3 You work in a department store.
.... you .... in a department store?

4 You know that man's name.
.... you .... that man's name?

Classic Extra page 101

16 A flat in London

Larry lives in a flat in London. That is the living room. There's a big chair near the window. Larry watches television in the evening here. There are no books here. Larry doesn't read them.

This is Larry's bedroom. He sleeps here. He watches television here, too.

That is the bathroom. Larry takes a shower here in the morning. There's a toilet here. There's a shower and a bath here, too.

This is Larry's kitchen. Larry eats breakfast and reads the newspaper here in the morning. He listens to the radio here, too. He doesn't eat a big breakfast: a cup of coffee and toast. That's all.

Vocabulary

1 Look.

| watch television | read a newspaper | drink coffee | eat toast | sleep | take a shower |

breakfast (morning)　　lunch (afternoon)　　dinner (evening)

2 Now answer the questions.

1 How many rooms are there in Larry's flat?
2 Where does Larry sleep?
3 Where does he watch television?
4 When does he take a shower?
5 What does he do in the kitchen?

3 Talk and write about yourself.

1 When do you watch television?
2 Where do you watch it?
3 Do you read a newspaper? When? Where?
4 Do you listen to the radio? When? Where?
5 Do you take a shower or a bath? When?

I watch television　　in the morning.
I read a newspaper　　in the afternoon.
　　　　　　　　　　　　in the evening.

I listen to the radio
I take a shower　　in the living room.
I work　　　　　　in the kitchen.
I drink...　　　　　in the...

Grammar

4 Look.

He	lives doesn't live	in London. in Oxford.

I	understand don't understand	this word. that word.

5 Complete these sentences.

1 Larry reads newspapers but he <u>doesn't read</u> books.
2 Diana likes Italian food but she _____ _____ English food.
3 She understands English but she _____ _____ Japanese.
4 Larry and Diana drink wine, but they _____ _____ it in the morning.
5 I know the answer to this question but I _____ the answer to that question.

Pronunciation

6 Listen and say the words.

1 wh<u>o</u>, tw<u>o</u>, r<u>oo</u>m
2 kn<u>ow</u>, <u>o</u>pen, cl<u>o</u>sed
3 <u>ea</u>t, sl<u>ee</u>p, <u>e</u>vening
4 b<u>e</u>d, r<u>e</u>d, br<u>ea</u>kfast
5 d<u>ay</u>, newsp<u>a</u>per, r<u>a</u>dio

Classic Extra page 101

17

Can you hear me ?

1 Answer the questions.

1 Can Shirley hear Jack?
2 Can he hear her?
3 Where is he?
4 Where is she?
5 What can he see?
6 Can she see them, too?

A detective is in Larry Jasper's flat. Another detective is in a car in the street.

SHIRLEY	Can you hear me, Jack?
JACK	Yes. I can.
SHIRLEY	Which room are you in?
JACK	The kitchen.
SHIRLEY	Is the door open or closed?
JACK	It's closed.
SHIRLEY	Open it.
JACK	All right. The door is open now.
SHIRLEY	Can you see the doors to the other rooms?
JACK	Yes, I can see them.
SHIRLEY	Good. Open the door to the living room.
JACK	Which door is that? I can see four doors.
SHIRLEY	I don't know. You can see them. I can't.

2 What about you?

1 Are you in a room?
2 Where is your teacher now? In front of you? Behind you? On your right? On your left?
3 Can you see a window?
4 Is it open or closed?
5 What can you see from the window?

3 Listen to Jack and Shirley. Answer the questions.

1 Which room is Jack in now?
2 What can he see?
3 Where is the photograph?
4 Jack can see a man's name. What is that name?

Vocabulary

4 Look.

He **can hear** her,
but he **can't see** her.

He **can see** her now,
but he **can't hear** her.

Open the door, please.

The door **is open** now.

Now **close** the door, please.

The door **is closed** now.

5 Look at this picture and answer the questions.

Hello, Susan.   *Hello, Bernard.*

1 Can he see her?   3 Can she see him?
2 Can he hear her?   4 Can she hear him?

Grammar

6 Look.

I	you	she	he	it	we	they
me	you	her	him	it	us	them

Where is she? he? it?

Where are they?

Where are you?

Down here.

Can you see her? him? it? them?

I can see you. Can you see me?

No.

7 Write the answers.

1 Can you see Larry?

No, I _can't_ see _him_ . Where is _he_ ?

2 Can you see Diana?

No, I _____ see _____ . Where is

_____ ?

3 Can you see Larry and Diana?

No, I _____ see _____ .

Where _____ ?

4 Can you see that man?

Yes, I _____ see _____ .

5 Can you see all that money?

No, I _____ see _____ .

Where _____ ?

Classic Extra page 102

18 More about Bernard

Bernard works in a museum in Oxford. It is open six days a week, from Tuesday to Sunday.

He usually gets up at six thirty. He starts work at nine and finishes at six or six thirty. He works from Monday to Friday. Monday is always a good day for him to work. The museum is closed on Monday.

He always eats lunch in a restaurant on Thursday. After work, he usually reads or listens to music. He never watches television, but sometimes he goes to the cinema. He sometimes goes to the opera or to concerts, too. He likes jazz and classical music very much. He plays the violin.

On Saturday he goes shopping in the morning. He often goes to London on Saturday afternoon. He sees friends there. He likes to talk to them.

1 Answer the questions.

1 Where does Bernard work?
2 Is the museum open seven days a week?
3 What time does he start work?
4 What time does he finish?
5 When does he have lunch in a restaurant?
6 What does he do in the evening?
7 What kind of music does he like?
8 What about Saturday afternoon? What does he do then?

2 What about you?

1 What time do you usually get up?
2 Do you often have lunch in a restaurant?
3 Do you often have dinner in a restaurant?
4 Do you watch television in the evening?
5 Do you go shopping very often?
6 Do you go shopping on Saturday?
7 What would you like to do after this lesson?
8 What do you like doing in the evening?

Vocabulary

3 **Look.** Go. Come.

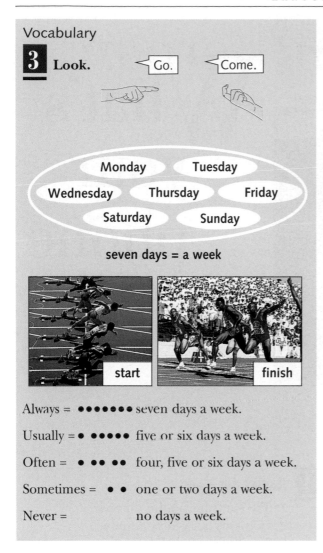

Monday   Tuesday
Wednesday   Thursday   Friday
Saturday   Sunday

seven days = a week

start   finish

Always = ●●●●●●● seven days a week.

Usually = ● ●●●●● five or six days a week.

Often = ● ●● ●● four, five or six days a week.

Sometimes = ● ● one or two days a week.

Never = no days a week.

4 **Talk and write about yourself.**

always	get up at…
usually	eat lunch in a restaurant.
I often	watch television in the evening.
sometimes	
never	listen to the radio in the morning.
	go to the cinema on Saturday.

usually…
I never…
always…

Grammar

5 **Look at these questions and answers.**

What does Bernard do at six thirty?
He gets up.
Where does he work?
In a museum.
When is the museum open?
From Tuesday to Sunday.

6 **Write the questions with 'what', 'where' or 'when'.**

1 *Where* does Bernard live?
In Oxford.

2 _____ does he do in the evening?
He reads or listens to music.

3 _____ does he work?
In a museum.

4 _____ is the museum closed?
On Monday.

5 _____ does he usually do in the evening?
He reads.

6 _____ does he go shopping?
On Saturday afternoons.

7 **Complete the questions. Then ask other people.**

When _____ you usually
get up?
eat breakfast?
go shopping?
watch television?
listen to the radio?

What do you usually _____ in the
morning?
afternoon?
evening?

Where do you usually
_____ breakfast?
_____ television?
_____ to the radio?
_____ lunch?

Classic Extra page 102

19

What's your phone number?

A man and a woman are in a café in London.

LARRY   What's your phone number, Diana?

DIANA   Pardon?

LARRY   I'd like your phone number.

DIANA   I don't understand.

LARRY   You don't understand?

DIANA   No. I don't understand.

LARRY   You don't understand the words "I'd like your phone number"?

DIANA   No, I don't understand why.

LARRY   Why?

DIANA   Yes. Why do you want it?

LARRY   Because I want to phone you.

DIANA   But why do you want to phone me?

LARRY   I don't want to talk about it now. Can you give it to me?

DIANA   What?

LARRY   Your phone number.

1   **Right or wrong?**

1 She wants his phone number.

2 He wants her phone number.

3 She doesn't understand the words "I'd like your phone number".

4 She wants to phone him.

5 He wants to phone her.

2   **Larry and Diana say more. Listen to them and answer the questions.**

1 What is Diana's phone number?

2 What is a good time to phone her?

3   **What about you?**

1 What is a good time to phone you?

2 Do you often phone people in the evening?

3 What are two things you often do in the evening?

Vocabulary

4 Look.

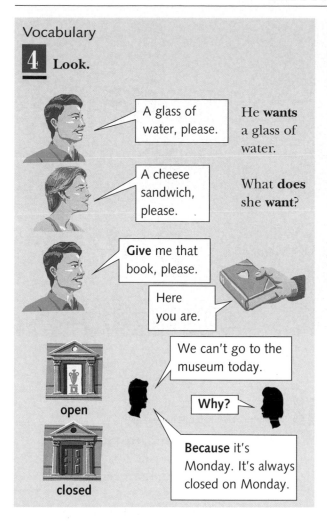

A glass of water, please.

He **wants** a glass of water.

A cheese sandwich, please.

What **does** she **want**?

Give me that book, please.

Here you are.

We can't go to the museum today.

open

Why?

closed

Because it's Monday. It's always closed on Monday.

5 Look at the pictures. Then complete the sentences below.

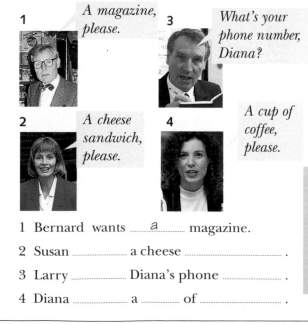

1 A magazine, please.

3 What's your phone number, Diana?

2 A cheese sandwich, please.

4 A cup of coffee, please.

1 Bernard wants ___a___ magazine.

2 Susan _____ a cheese _____ .

3 Larry _____ Diana's phone _____ .

4 Diana _____ a _____ of _____ .

Grammar

6 Look.

I You We They	live in... like... work... understand...	I You We They	**don't**	live in... like... work...
He She	lives in... likes... works...	He She	**doesn't**	live in... like... work...

7 Complete the sentences.

1 Does Larry live in Oxford?

No, he _doesn't live_ in Oxford. He
lives in London.

2 Does Bernard live in London?

No, he _____ live in London. He
_____ in Oxford.

3 Does Diana like English food?

No, she _____ English food.
She _____ Italian food.

4 Do you understand this book?

No, I _____ all of it, but I
_____ some of it.

5 Do you usually get up at 3 o'clock?

No, I _____ usually _____ up at
3 o'clock. I usually _____ up at
_____ .

6 Do you usually drink champagne?

No, I _____ usually _____
champagne. I usually _____ .

Pronunciation

8 Listen and say the words.

1 wh<u>o</u>, f<u>oo</u>d, t<u>oo</u>, tw<u>o</u>, d<u>o</u>
2 c<u>u</u>p, b<u>u</u>s, d<u>oe</u>s, d<u>oe</u>sn't
3 g<u>o</u>, n<u>o</u>, kn<u>ow</u>, ph<u>o</u>ne, d<u>o</u>n't

Classic Extra page 103

20

Have you got the time?

A man and a woman are on a train.

MAN Have you got the time?

SUSAN Yes. It's six fifty.

MAN Six fifteen?

SUSAN No. Six fifty. Ten to seven.

MAN Thank you.

SUSAN You're welcome.

MAN Are you American?

SUSAN No. Why?

MAN Because Americans say "You're welcome" when people say "thank you" and because you've got an American accent.

SUSAN No, I haven't. I've got a Canadian accent.

MAN But a Canadian accent and an American accent are the same, aren't they?

SUSAN No. They're different.

MAN Are they? I can't hear the difference.

SUSAN No, perhaps you can't. But there is a small difference.

1 Answer the questions.

1 What do Americans often say when people say "thank you"?
2 Why does the man think Susan is an American?
3 What kind of accent has Susan got?
4 Are American and Canadian English accents the same? Or is there a difference?

2 The young man on the train answers some questions. Listen and answer these questions.

1 What is his first name?
2 Where is he from?
3 Where does he live now?
4 Does he like it there?
5 What are three good things there?
6 Where does he work?

Vocabulary

3 Look.

The **same** time,
the **same** clocks.

The **same** time,
different clocks.

Larry **has got** a big car.

I've got a big car.

We usually say "He's got ...", "She's got...". and "I've got...". Here, 's means 'has' and 've means 'have'.

WELCOME TO OXFORD

You can say **welcome to...** when people come to your country or town.

4 Say a word on the left. Then say the opposite on the right.

good	*after*
cheap	*old*
rich	*expensive*
same	*last*
always	*close*
go	*poor*
open	*never*
start	*bad*
before	*come*
first	*different*
new	*finish*

Grammar

5 Look.

We write:

He She It	**has**	got...
I We You They	**have**	got...

We say:

He She It	**'s**	got...
I We You They	**'ve**	got...

6 **Ask other people these questions.**

Have you got...?

Yes, I have.

No, I haven't.

a car	a camera	a bike	a dog

a light	a watch	a pen	a cat

Pronunciation

7 **Say the words. Is the sound the same or different?**

good, book — The same.

good, dog — Different.

1 b**oo**k, l**oo**k   5 g**o**, d**o**
2 g**oo**d, f**oo**d   6 g**oes**, cl**o**se
3 w**o**man, w**o**men   7 g**oes**, d**oes**
4 cl**o**se, kn**ows**   8 d**o**, d**oes**

📼 **Now listen. Are you right?**

Classic Extra page 103

Progress Check 2 Units 11-20

He	**lives**	in London.
She	**sells**	cars.
	comes	from Australia.

I	**live**	in a flat.
We	**like**	good food.
You	**work**	five days a week.

Questions

Does	he	**live**	in London?
	she	**sell**	cars?
	she	**come**	from Australia?

Do	you	**live**	in a flat, too?
	they	**like**	Italian food, too?
		work	in an office, too?

Negatives

He	**doesn't**	**live**	in Liverpool.
She		**sell**	food.
		come	from England.

I	**don't**	**live**	in a big house.
You		**like**	this kind of food.
We		**work**	on Sunday.
They			

Monday   Tuesday
Wednesday   Thursday   Friday
Saturday   Sunday

●●●●●●●

●●●●●●● always
●●● ●●● usually
● ●● ●● often
● ● sometimes
never

I	get up before seven.
He	sees Larry in the café.
She	sees him there, too.
You	drink champagne.
We	drink tea in the morning.

I	**'m**	here.
He	**'s**	here, too.
She	**'s**	there.
It	**'s**	here.

My	name	is	Bernard.
His			Diana.
Her			Larry.
Its			Paddington.

They	can	see	**me.**
		hear	**him.**
			her.
			it.

We	**'re**	in London.
You	**'re**	in Paris.
They	**'re**	in the park.

Our	names	are	in the book.
Your	address	is	here.
Their	address		here, too.

Can	she	see	**us?**
		see	**you?**
		hear	**them?**

in

on

at

In	the morning.
	afternoon.
	evening.

On	Monday.
	Tuesday.
	Wednesday.

At	three	o'clock.
	four	
	five	
	night.	

Now test yourself!

1 What are the answers? Write A–G.

1 What is Larry's last name? `B`

2 What does he do?

3 Where does he live?

4 When does he get up?

5 What does he do in the evening?

6 When does he take a bath?

7 Why doesn't he read books?

A He usually watches television.

B Jasper.

C He buys and sells cars.

D He isn't interested in them.

E In a flat near Victoria Station.

F He doesn't. But he takes a shower in the morning.

G Usually at seven thirty in the morning.

2 Write the words 'does', 'do', 'doesn't', 'don't', 'work', 'works' or 'lives'.

1 Diana Brentano _lives_ in a flat.

2 Where .... Larry live?

3 What about you? Where .... you live?

4 Bernard Winter is an art expert. He .... in a museum in Oxford.

5 Do you .... in a museum?

6 Susan Farr .... work in a museum. She is a journalist.

7 Diana and Larry .... work in a museum. He buys and sells cars and she is a make-up artist.

3 Write the questions.

1 I live in England.
   Do you live in England, too?

2 I can see a plane. .... you .... a plane, too?

3 Diana likes Italian food. ....
   she .... English food, too?

4 Bernard goes shopping on Saturday.
   .... you ....
   shopping ...., too?

5 Larry watches television in the evening.
   .... Bernard .... television
   ...., too?

4 Write negative sentences.

1 Bernard lives in Oxford.
   Larry _doesn't live_ in Oxford.

2 Larry buys and sells cars.
   Bernard .... and
   .... cars.

3 Bernard likes classical music.
   Larry .... classical music.

4 Larry and Bernard are English.
   Susan and Diana .... English.

5 Some people like big cities but some people .... them.

5 What is the next word?

1 I can see him. Can you see _him?_

2 The door is open. Please close ....

3 I don't like cats. Do you like ....

4 I don't like Larry. Do you like ....

5 I can't see Diana. Can you see ....

21 Two families

Susan's mother and father live in Toronto. Her father's name is Tom. Her mother's name is Barbara Farr.

Susan has got a brother and a sister. His name is Robert and her name is Laura. Laura is married. She's got one child, a girl.

Robert is married, too. His wife's name is Margaret. They haven't got any children. Susan isn't married. She is single.

Doris and Joe O'Hara live in Toronto, too. They have got two sons, Bill and Frank.

Bill is married to Susan's sister. Frank is married, too. His wife's name is Sonia and they have got two children, a boy and a girl. Their daughter's name is Linda and their son's name is George.

1 Right or wrong?

1 Tom Farr is Susan's father and Barbara Farr is her mother.
2 Susan has got two sisters and one brother.
3 Susan's sister is married but her brother is single.
4 Susan's brother hasn't got any children but her sister has got one child.
5 Laura's husband is Bill O'Hara.
6 Bill has got a brother but he hasn't got a sister.
7 Doris O'Hara is Sonia's mother and Joe is her father.
8 Sonia is Frank's wife.
9 They have got two sons.

2 What about you?

1 How many brothers or sisters have you got?
2 What are their names?
3 Where do they live?
4 Are you married or single?
5 How many children have you got?

Vocabulary

3 Look.

A family

husband · wife · father · mother · son · daughters · brother · sisters

Any: We say **any** in questions and negatives: "Have you got any children?" "Margaret and Robert haven't got any children."

DORIS O'HARA · JOE O'HARA

They are **married**.
They are **husband** and **wife**.
The opposite of married is **single**.
Single means 'not married'.

Children

KAREN · GEORGE · LINDA · TOM FARR

a child (a girl) · a child (a boy) · young · old

Pronunciation

4 In which word is the sound different?

1 wife, five, (children,) child
2 single, different, children, child
3 husband, mother, woman, young
4 woman, brother, book

Now say the words with these sounds:

1 'i' in five   3 'i' in children
2 'u' in husband 4 'oo' in good

Grammar

5 Look.

He's She's	got	a...	Has	he she	got a...?
I've You've	got	a...	Have	I you	got a...?

6 Ask questions about Susan. What are the answers?

a brother?
Has Susan got a sister?
any children?

Yes, she has.
No, she hasn't.

7 Now ask other people.

Yes, I have.

sisters?
Have you got any brothers?
children?

No, I haven't.

8 Write two or three sentences about your family.

one sister.
one brother.
I've got one son.
two sons.
three daughters.

He/She lives in...
They live in...
Her name is...
His name is...
Their names are...

Classic Extra page 104

22

What do I get?

The man with Larry is Basil Newton.

BASIL   Do you understand my problem, Larry?

LARRY   Yes, I understand your problem, Basil. You want a picture. The picture is in a museum. The museum doesn't want to sell the picture.

BASIL   Well? Can you get the picture for me?

LARRY   Yes, I think so, but what do I get from you?

BASIL   Money, Larry. A lot of money, Larry. You know that.

LARRY   How much money, Basil?

BASIL   Twenty-five thousand pounds.

LARRY   Twenty-five thousand. Hmm.

BASIL   Well? What's your answer?

LARRY   Give me time, Basil.

BASIL   Give you time? Why?

LARRY   Because I want to think about it. That's why.

1   Right or wrong?

1 Basil wants a picture.
2 Larry has got the picture.
3 Larry thinks he can get the picture.
4 The picture is in a museum now.
5 Basil can buy the picture from the museum.

2   Answer the questions. The answer for one of the questions here is "I don't know". Which question is it?

1 What does Basil want?
2 Where is the picture now?
3 What is the problem?
4 How much money does Larry want?

3   Listen to more of Basil's and Larry's conversation. Then answer the questions.

1 How much time does Larry want to think about it?
2 When can Basil have Larry's answer?
3 What is Basil's new telephone number?

Vocabulary

4 Look.

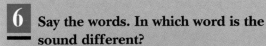

give →   ← get

The word 'get' can mean different things. How many different meanings are here?

A Where can I **get** a newspaper?
B Can we **get** a bus from here to Oxford?
C I **get** a lot of letters every day.
D Please **get** me a glass of water.
E Can I **get** a ticket to Oxford here?
F I want to **get** the ten o'clock train to London.

5 Answer the questions.

1 In two of the six sentences above, 'get' means 'buy'. Which two sentences are they? ☐ ☐

2 Look at C. Can you find another sentence with the same meaning of 'get'? ☐

3 A friend says to you: "Please get me a doctor." What do you do?

Pronunciation

6 Say the words. In which word is the sound different?

1 three, think, (this,) thanks
2 that, them, then, third
3 thirty, thousand, bath, father
4 they, brother, mother, month
5 weather, other, fourth, their

🔊 **Listen. Are you right? Now listen and say all the words with the 'th' sound in three; then say the 'th' sound in this.**

Grammar

7 Look.

How	much	water ? money ? time?
How	many	hours? minutes? days? months? years? glasses of water? American dollars? English pounds?

8 Answer these questions.

1 How many hours do you work every day?
2 How much time have you got for English today?
3 How much coffee do you drink in a day?
4 How many cigarettes do you smoke in a day?

9 Complete these questions.

1 How _much_ coffee do you drink in a day?
2 How .... money have you got now?
3 How .... brothers have you got?
4 How .... sisters have you got?
5 How .... beer or wine do you usually drink in the evening?
6 How .... people are there in the room with you now?

10 Ask other people the questions in Exercise 9. What are their answers?

Classic Extra page 104

23

Who are they?

Tony Stuart is a waiter. He works in a restaurant in Oxford. He is tall and thin. He's got dark hair. He's twenty-four years old and he loves a beautiful young woman. Her name is Juliet. She's got long, fair hair and he thinks she is very beautiful. Her father is very rich.

Maureen Murphy is thirty years old. She works in a musum in Oxford. She is tall and has got fair hair.

Basil Newton hasn't got very much hair now. It's grey. He isn't tall and he isn't short. He's fifty-five years old and he's Juliet's father.

Harry is thirty-one years old. He's got short, dark hair. He isn't fat but he isn't very thin. He's married to Maureen.

1 **Look at the people in picture one. Which questions can you answer about them?**

1 What are their names?
2 How old are they?
3 What can you say about their hair?
4 What does one of them do?

Now talk about the people in the other pictures. What can you say about them?

2 **Listen to two people.**

1 Who are the two people?
2 One of the two people says "I don't want to talk about him". Who is 'him'?
3 Does she like him?
4 Does she love him?

Vocabulary

3 **Look.**

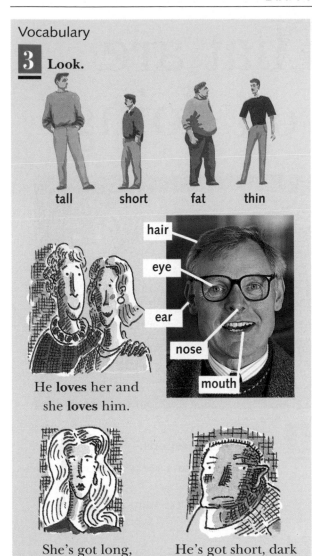

tall   short   fat   thin

hair

eye

ear

nose

mouth

He **loves** her and
she **loves** him.

She's got long,
fair hair and
she's **beautiful**.

He's got short, dark
hair and he's **ugly**.

4 Talk about someone, but don't say his
or her name. Can other people say who
it is?

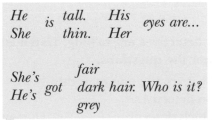

He   is tall.   His   eyes are...
She   thin. Her

She's   fair
He's got dark hair. Who is it?
          grey

I think it's...

Pronunciation

5 **In which word is the sound different?**

1 b<u>eau</u>tiful, J<u>u</u>liet, m<u>u</u>seum, m<u>u</u>ch
2 l<u>o</u>ve, m<u>u</u>ch, m<u>o</u>ney, d<u>o</u>n't
3 th<u>ere</u>, h<u>air</u>, h<u>ere</u>, wh<u>ere</u>
4 d<u>au</u>ghter, w<u>a</u>ter, t<u>a</u>ll, It<u>a</u>ly

Listen. Say the words with the sounds:

1 'eau' in b<u>eau</u>tiful   3 'air' in h<u>air</u>
2 'u' in m<u>u</u>ch   4 'a' in w<u>a</u>ter

Grammar

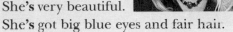

6 **Study these
sentences with 's.**

Juliet is Basil**'s**
daughter.
She**'s** very beautiful.
She**'s** got big blue eyes and fair hair.

1 A different way of saying sentence one
is "Juliet is the daughter **of** Basil".
2 In sentence two, **'s** means 'is'.
3 In sentence three, **'s** means 'has'.

We often say:	But we write:
She's... He's... He's got... She's got...	She is... He is... He has got... She has got...

7 **Now write 'is' or 'has'.**

1 Who's that? _is_

2 That's Tony. ....

3 He's got short dark hair. ....

4 He's very tall. ....

5 He's got blue eyes, too. ....

6 He's a waiter. ....

7 He's very thin. ....

8 He's got two sisters. ....

Classic Extra page 105

24

What are you doing?

It's seven o'clock in the evening.

LARRY	Hello, Diana. This is Larry. How are you?
DIANA	I'm all right.
LARRY	What are you doing?
DIANA	I'm watching television.
LARRY	Oh. Are you near a window?
DIANA	Yes.
LARRY	Look out of it. Can you see a big car in the street?
DIANA	Why are you asking me all these questions?
LARRY	Because I'm in that big car. And I'd like to talk to you about money.
DIANA	Money?
LARRY	Yes. Are you interested?
DIANA	Yes, I am, but why can't you...
LARRY	I'm waiting for you. Are you coming?
DIANA	Yes.

1 Answer the questions.

1 What can Diana see from her window?
2 Who is in the car?
3 What does Larry want to talk about?

2 What about you?

1 Are you near a window?
2 Look out of the window. What can you see?
3 Are you interested in money?
4 What are two other things you are interested in?
5 Do you watch television?
6 Are you watching television now?

3 Two detectives are talking. Listen and answer the questions.

1 What are the names of the two detectives?
2 Which detective is in a car? The man or the woman?
3 Who is the detective watching?
4 Where exactly is the detective's car?

Vocabulary

4 **Look.**

We say **these** when the things are very near you.
We say **those** when they aren't very near.

These things.

Those things.

Pronunciation

5 **Say the words. In which word is the sound different?**

1 h<u>ow</u>, n<u>ow</u>, (kn<u>ow</u>,) h<u>ou</u>se
2 kn<u>ow</u>, g<u>o</u>, d<u>o</u>, wind<u>ow</u>
3 w<u>ai</u>t, n<u>a</u>me, <u>eigh</u>t, w<u>a</u>tch
4 f<u>ir</u>st, g<u>ir</u>l, w<u>or</u>k, Vict<u>o</u>ria

 Now listen. Are you right?

Grammar

6 **Look.**

What **are** you doing?

I'**m** work**ing**.

This question means "What are you doing now?" In questions, 'am, is, are' come before 'I, you, he, she, we, they'.

I	am	doing...
He She It	is	going... watching... waiting...
You We They	are	talking... eating... drinking...

7 **Answer the questions.**

1 The man in this picture works in an office. But what is he doing? Is he working now?

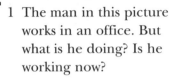

2 The woman in this picture is waiting for a bus. Can you see the bus? Is it coming now?

8 **Complete the questions and answers.**

What ___are___ you doing?

I'm _____ television.

What _____ you doing?

I'm _____ing a book.

Where _____ you _____ ?

To work.

Classic Extra page 105

25 What are they doing?

Two detectives are talking.

JACK	What are you doing now, Shirley?
SHIRLEY	I'm watching Larry and Diana. I can see them but they can't see me.
JACK	Where are they?
SHIRLEY	They're in a restaurant. They're sitting very near the window.
JACK	What are they doing?
SHIRLEY	He's talking. She's listening and she's looking at something in his hand.
JACK	Something? What?
SHIRLEY	I think it's a photograph. Yes, it is. I'm not sure, but I think it's a photograph of a person.
JACK	Is it a man or a woman?
SHIRLEY	I don't know. I can't see. I'm going now.
JACK	Wait! Where are you going?
SHIRLEY	Into the restaurant.
JACK	But why?
SHIRLEY	I want to look at that photograph. That's why!

1 Answer the questions.

1 What is Shirley doing?
2 Where is she?
3 Where are Larry and Diana?
4 What are they doing?
5 Where is Shirley going?
6 What does she want to do?

2 What about you?

1 What are you doing now?
2 Are you sitting or standing?
3 Look at someone near you. What is he or she doing?
4 What do you want to do after the lesson?

Vocabulary

3 Look.

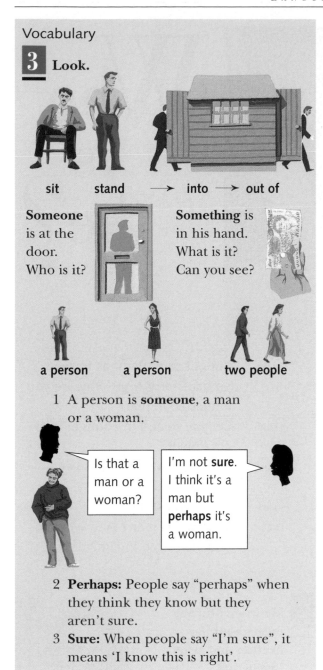

sit   stand   → into → out of

Someone is at the door. Who is it?

Something is in his hand. What is it? Can you see?

a person   a person   two people

1 A person is **someone**, a man or a woman.

> Is that a man or a woman?

> I'm not **sure**. I think it's a man but **perhaps** it's a woman.

2 **Perhaps:** People say "perhaps" when they think they know but they aren't sure.

3 **Sure:** When people say "I'm sure", it means 'I know this is right'.

4 Say the word on the left. The other person says the opposite of that word.

dark	*single*
married	*short*
beautiful	*listen*
expensive	*fair*
on	*fat*
talk	*ugly*
thin	*off*
tall	*cheap*

Grammar

5 Look.

> **Do** they **do** it?
> **Are** they **doing** it now?
>
> Larry and Diana **drink** wine.
> They **are drinking** wine now.

6 Look at the picture and the questions. You can give four different answers.

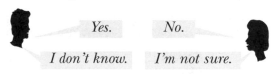

Yes.   *No.*

I don't know.   *I'm not sure.*

1 Is Diana drinking wine?
2 Does she smoke?
3 Is she smoking?
4 Is Larry smoking?
5 Does he watch television?
6 Is he watching television?
7 Does Larry drink whisky?
8 Are they drinking whisky?

7 What about you?

1 Do you smoke?
2 Do you drink coffee?
3 Do you watch television?
4 Do you read English?
5 Do you speak English?
6 What are you doing now?

Classic Extra page 106

26

Who is he?

LARRY	Look at this man's hair and my hair. What's the difference?
DIANA	Your hair is a little darker.
LARRY	What about his eyes?
DIANA	They're the same colour as your eyes. Who is this man, Larry?
LARRY	How old is he?
DIANA	I don't know. Why are you asking me?
LARRY	How old do you think he is?

DIANA	I'm not sure. Perhaps forty, perhaps forty-one. Why are you interested in him?
LARRY	Do you think I'm younger? Or am I older?
DIANA	I don't know! Now answer my questions.
LARRY	Which questions?
DIANA	Who is this man? And why are you interested in him?

1 **Answer the questions with these words.**

I don't know.

I have no idea.

I'm not sure but I think...

Yes.   *No.*

1 Is Larry younger than Bernard? Is he older? Or are they the same age?
2 Do you think Diana is a lot younger than Larry? Or is she a little younger? Or do you think she is the same age?
3 Is Diana's hair the same colour as your hair?
4 Is her hair longer than your hair? Or is it shorter?

2 **Maureen Murphy talks about her brother and sister. Listen and answer the questions.**

1 What are the names of her brother and sister?
2 How old are they?
3 Which one is younger than Maureen?
4 Which one is older?
5 Are they taller than Maureen?
6 What colour eyes has her sister got?

Vocabulary

3 **Look.**

Bernard	Susan	Dominic	Larry
40	37	5	40

1 Dominic is **younger** than Larry.
2 Larry is **a lot older** than Dominic.
3 Bernard is **a little older** than Susan.
4 Bernard and Larry are **the same age**.
5 Larry is **taller** than Dominic.
6 Dominic is **shorter** than Larry.

4 **Answer the questions.**

1 Who is older?
   Tony? Or Basil?
2 Who is taller?
3 Who do you
   think is richer?
4 Do you think
   Tony is a lot
   younger than
   Basil? Or only a
   little younger?

Pronunciation

5 **Say the words. Is the sound the same or different?**

daughter, tall   [The same.]
1 sure, she
2 sure, poor
3 poor, book
4 door, daughter

▭ **Now listen. Are you right?**

Grammar

6 **Look.**

He She	is	younger older shorter taller richer	than	me. Susan. him. her. you.

7 **Complete these questions.**

1 Are you (young) than Dominic?

   younger

2 Are you (old) than Tony?
3 Are you (tall) than him, too?
4 Basil Newton has got a lot of money.
   Do you think he is (rich) than you?
5 Dominic is five. Is he a lot (young) or
   only a little (young) than you?

8 **Ask other people questions.**

 Is Dominic | older younger taller shorter | *than you?*

He's | a lot a little | older younger taller shorter | *than me.*

9 **Now write four sentences about yourself.**

I think I am | a little a lot | younger older taller shorter | than Dominic.

Classic Extra page 106

27

Today and tomorrow

It is Wednesday evening. Bernard Winter often works late on Wednesday evening.

He is going to work late this evening. There are a lot of letters and other things on his desk.

Tomorrow is Thursday. Bernard is going to talk to some students in the morning. After that, he is going to see a journalist.

All these things are in Bernard's diary, but the diary isn't on his desk. It's on his secretary's desk.

Bernard always has lunch in a restaurant on Thursday. The restaurant is called Ricardo's Table. It is near the museum.

1 Right or wrong?

1 Bernard's diary is on his desk in front of him.
2 Bernard is talking to some students now.
3 He is going to talk to them tomorrow.
4 He is also going to see a journalist.
5 First he going to see the journalist. Then he is going to see the students.
6 He is going to have lunch at work tomorrow.

2 What about you?

1 Have you got a diary?
2 What are you going to do tomorrow? Do you know?
3 Where are you going to have lunch tomorrow? In a restaurant? At home? At work? At school?
4 What are you going to do after this lesson? Go home? See some friends? Have a drink? Watch television? Work?
5 What are three things you are going to do next week?

Vocabulary

3 Look.

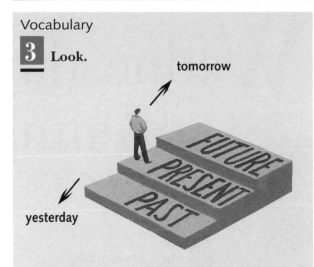

1 **Today** is now. Today is in the present.
2 **Yesterday** was the day before today. Yesterday is in the past.
3 **Tomorrow** is the day after today. Tomorrow is the future.

4 **Going to:** When we talk about the future, we often say **going to**: "It's going to rain."
5 **Late** means after the time you usually do something: "Bernard usually finishes work at six, but this evening he is going to work late. He is going to finish after six." The opposite is **early**: "I'm going to get up early tomorrow."

Pronunciation

4 Say three words with the same sound as 1–4.

1 cl**o**ck   2 h**er**   3 **u**p   4 n**o**se

w**or**k, wh**a**t, **ear**ly, tom**o**rrow
m**o**ther, m**o**nth, cl**o**se, d**oe**s
kn**ow**s, g**oe**s, g**o**t, j**ou**rnalist

 Now listen. Are you right?

Grammar

5 Look.

Tomorrow...

I	am		have dinner at eight.
he	is		watch television.
she		(not) **going to**	buy some food.
you			see a film.
we	are		read the newspaper.
they			write some letters.

6 Read about Basil. Then say sentences about yourself.

1 He's going to have lunch in a restaurant tomorrow.

I'm going to have lunch in a restaurant, too.

Basil

I'm not going to have lunch in a restaurant. I'm going to have lunch at home.

You

2 He's going to get up at ten o'clock tomorrow.
3 He's going to have a very big breakfast.
4 He's going to have lunch in a very expensive restaurant.
5 He's going to smoke five or six cigarettes tomorrow.
6 Tomorrow evening he's going to have a bottle of champagne with his dinner.
7 He's going to watch television in the evening.

7 Write five sentences about yourself.

Tomorrow...

*I am (not) going to eat in a restaurant.
going to watch television.
drink champagne.
eat meat.*

Classic Extra page 107

28

Wednesday evening

1 What do you think?
Answer these questions.

1 What is Bernard going to do this evening?
2 Is Maureen going to do it, too?
3 When is Bernard going to talk to some students?
4 What is he going to do at eleven o'clock?

Maureen Murphy is Bernard Winter's secretary.

MAUREEN I'm going home now, Bernard. Are you going to work late?

BERNARD Yes, I am. Goodbye, Maureen. Oh, just a moment, please. What about tomorrow? What's in my diary?

MAUREEN Well, some students are coming to see you tomorrow morning. At ten o'clock. And then that journalist wants to speak to you at eleven o'clock.

BERNARD That journalist? Which journalist?

MAUREEN Her name is Susan Farr. She's from Canada.

BERNARD Why does she want to see me?

MAUREEN She explains all that in her letter. Don't you remember?

BERNARD In her letter? Which letter?

MAUREEN It's one of those letters in front of you now, Bernard.

2 What about you?

1 When are you going home?
2 What are you going to do tomorrow afternoon?
3 What are you going to do tomorrow evening?

3 Larry Jasper is talking to Diana on the phone. Listen and answer the questions.

1 What time is it?
2 When does Larry want to see Diana?
3 Where does he want to see her?

Vocabulary

 Look.

What's her name?

I can't remember.

1 **Remember:** The man does not know her name now. He does not **remember** it. The opposite of 'remember' is 'forget'.

2 **Wait just a moment** means 'Wait a few seconds'.

3 **A student** is someone at a university or some kind of school.

4 **Speak** means 'say things, talk': "How many languages do you speak?"

5 **Explain:** English teachers often **explain** words to their students. A student can say: "I don't understand this word. Can you explain it to me, please?"

6 **A letter** is something you write to another person.

Pronunciation

 What are the words with the same sound?

diary, speak, English, weight,
late, why, people, give,
women, explain, light, these

1 Say three words with the same sound as s<u>ee</u>.

2 Say three words with the same sound as th<u>i</u>s.

3 Say three words with the same sound as s<u>ay</u>.

4 Say three words with the same sound as f<u>i</u>ve.

📼 **Now listen. Are you right?**

Grammar

Look at these questions about tomorrow.

> It is raining now.
> **Is** it **going to** rain tomorrow, too?

> We are late.
> **Are** we **going to** be late tomorrow, too?

Read the sentences. Change them into questions about tomorrow.

1 Bernard is working late today.

<u>Is</u> he going to <u>work</u> late tomorrow, too?

2 We are speaking English. .... we

.... to speak English tomorrow, too?

3 Two detectives are watching Larry now.

.... they .... to .... him

tomorrow, too?

4 Susan is interviewing someone now.

.... she .... interview

someone tomorrow, ...?

5 Basil is eating in a very expensive

restaurant. ....

.... in a very expensive

.... tomorrow, ...?

6 You are reading this book now. ....

.... it

tomorrow, too?

Ask other people questions.

Are you going to

Yes, I am.

work late
come here
watch television
speak English

tomorrow?

No, I'm not.

Classic Extra page 107

29

The answer

Larry Jasper and Basil Newton are talking again.

BASIL   When can you get that picture for me?

LARRY   Soon.

BASIL   How soon? Tomorrow? The day after tomorrow? On Friday? On Saturday? When?

LARRY   Tomorrow.

BASIL   I see. You're going to get the picture tomorrow.

LARRY   Just a moment, Basil. There's a problem.

BASIL   A problem? What?

LARRY   It isn't going to be easy to get that picture from the museum. It's going to be difficult! Very difficult.

BASIL   I know that, Larry. That's why I'm going to pay you twenty-five thousand.

LARRY   That's the problem, Basil. Twenty-five thousand isn't enough. I want more than that.

1 Answer the questions.
For one question here, the answer is "I don't know". Which one?

1 When can Larry get the picture?
2 What is the problem?
3 How much more does Larry want?

2 What about you?

1 What are you going to do tomorrow?
2 What are you going to do the day after tomorrow?
3 What are two things you are going to do next Sunday?

3 Listen to the conversation. Then answer these questions.

1 How much money does Larry want?
2 Is Basil going to give it to him?
3 What is Basil going to do before Larry gets the painting?
4 What is Basil going to do after Larry gets the painting?

Vocabulary

4 **Look.**

1 **Soon:** Not long from now.
2 **Easy/Difficult:**

This is **easy**. This is **difficult**.

3 **A problem** is something difficult.
4 **Enough:** You want to buy something. It costs £50. You've got £45. You haven't got **enough** money. That's a problem!
5 **More than:** "I want more than twenty-five thousand" means that twenty-five thousand is not enough.

5 **One of you says a word on the left. The other says the opposite on the right.**

easy	answer
goodbye	late
past	difficult
remember	forget
yesterday	hello
early	tomorrow
ask	future

Pronunciation

6 **Say the words. Is the sound the same or different?**

m<u>o</u>ney, b<u>u</u>s The same.

1 en<u>ou</u>gh, b<u>u</u>s
2 en<u>ou</u>gh, <u>fr</u>ont
3 en<u>ou</u>gh, th<u>ou</u>sand
4 th<u>ou</u>sand, h<u>ow</u>
5 s<u>oo</u>n, d<u>o</u>

 Now listen. Are you right?

Grammar

7 **Look.**

1 **On** + day: **On** Monday.
2 **At** + time: **At** three o'clock.
3 Remember! We don't say 'at' or 'on' with 'tomorrow':

| I am going to work | **on** Tuesday.
tomorrow. |

8 **Complete the sentences with 'on' or 'at'.**

1 Bernard usually starts work ___*at*___ nine.
2 He usually finishes _____ six.
3 But _____ Tuesday, he sometimes finishes _____ six thirty.
4 What are you going to do _____ Friday?
5 What do you usually do _____ Sunday?
6 Do you usually get up _____ six _____ Sunday?

9 **How many questions can you ask other people?**

Are you going to

speak English	tomorrow?
come here	the day after
get up early	tomorrow?
work late	on Monday?
start work at	on Tuesday?
nine o'clock	on Wednesday?

10 **What are you going to do? When are you going to do it? Write four sentences about yourself.**

I'm going to... on...
I'm not going to...
 tomorrow.
I'm going to...
 the day after tomorrow.
I'm not going to...
 the day after tomorrow.

Classic Extra page 108

30

How long are you staying?

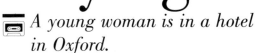 *A young woman is in a hotel in Oxford.*

GIRL Can I help you?

SUSAN Yes, my name is Susan Farr. I've got a reservation.

GIRL How do you spell your last name, please?

SUSAN F.A.R.R.

GIRL Yes, a single room with a shower. And you're going to stay for two nights. Is that right?

SUSAN Yes.

GIRL How would you like to pay?

SUSAN I have a credit card. Would you like to see it?

GIRL Yes, please.

SUSAN Here you are. Do you want to see my passport, too?

GIRL No. That isn't necessary. Would you like a newspaper in the morning?

SUSAN Yes, please.

GIRL Which one?

SUSAN 'The Times', please. Oh. What time is breakfast?

1 Answer the questions.

1 How long is Susan going to stay?
2 What kind of room is it?
3 What does the girl want to see?
4 Does she want to see Susan's passport, too?
5 What would Susan like in the morning?

2 What about you?

1 How do you spell your name?
2 When do you usually have breakfast?
3 Have you got a credit card?
4 Do people in your country pay with credit cards very often?

3 Listen and answer the questions.

1 What time is breakfast?
2 Where would Susan like to have breakfast?
3 Where can she have breakfast?
4 Is this the key to Susan's room?

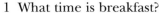

Vocabulary

4 Look.

1 **Reservation:** When you have a **reservation**, the hotel knows you are coming and you have a room: "The reservation is in the name of Winter."

2 **A single room** is a room for one person; a room for two people is called 'a double room'.

3 **Spell** means to say or write the letters in a word: "How do you spell the word 'necessary'? With one 's' or two?"

4 **Stay** means to live or be somewhere for a short time: "Susan lives in Canada but she is staying in Oxford for five days."

5 **Necessary:** Food is **necessary**. Water is **necessary**, too. With no food or water, you can't live. Coffee is nice, but it is not **necessary**.

6 **Pay** means to give money when you buy something.

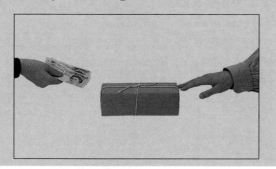

Pronunciation

5 Look at these words. One sound in them is the same. What is that sound?

nec<u>e</u>ssary, res<u>e</u>rvation, yest<u>e</u>rday, wom<u>a</u>n, <u>a</u>gain, t<u>o</u>morrow, breakf<u>a</u>st, probl<u>e</u>m, pict<u>u</u>re, diffic<u>u</u>lt, diff<u>e</u>rence, diff<u>e</u>rent, mom<u>e</u>nt, stud<u>e</u>nt, mus<u>eu</u>m, newspap<u>e</u>r, show<u>e</u>r, phot<u>o</u>graph, Saturd<u>a</u>y, tea <u>a</u>nd coffee, fish <u>a</u>nd chips

Now listen to the words. Say them.

Grammar

6 Look.

I He/She We/You They	'd	like to	buy a new car. have a cup of coffee. watch television. go home now.
Would	you he she	like to	have lunch? go to the cinema? sit here?

When we talk, we often say 'I'd... We'd...' etc. But in questions we say 'Would'.

7 Now talk about yourself. Say three or four things you'd like to do tomorrow.

I'd like to   *go shopping/buy a...*
have lunch in a good...
eat/drink...
have... for dinner.
go to... in the evening.

8 Perhaps other people would like to do the same things. Ask these questions.

Would you like to... tomorrow?

Yes, I would.

No, but I'd like to...

When would you like to...?

At...

9 Write three things you would like to do next week, next month or next year.

Next week I would like to see/watch/ listen to...
Next month I would like to go to...
Next year I would like to buy a...

Classic Extra page 108

Progress Check 3 Units 21-30

He She	**has got**	a good job. a lot of money.

I You They	**have got**	a good job. a lot of money.

Questions

Has	he she	**got**	a good job? a lot of money?

Have	I/you they	**got**	a good job? a lot of money?

Negatives

He She	**hasn't got**	a good job. any money.

I/You They	**haven't got**	a good job. any money.

He She	**is**	watching looking at listening to	them. you. us. me.

I	**am**	watching listening to looking at	them. him. her.
You We	**are**		

Questions

Is	he she	watching looking at listening to	you? us? me? them?

Am	I	listening to watching looking at	him? us? me? her?
Are	you they		

Negatives

He She	**isn't**	watching looking at listening to	him. them. you. us. me.

I	**'m not**	watching listening to looking at	them. him. her.
You We	**aren't**		

He She	**is**	**going to**	see Bernard. buy a new car. do it.

I You We	**am** **are**	**going to**	see it. buy it. do it.

Questions

Is	he she	**going to**	see Bernard? buy a new car? do it?

Are	you they	**going to**	see it? buy it? do it?

Negatives

He She	**isn't going to**	see Bernard. buy a new car. do it.

I You We	**'m not** **aren't**	**going to**	see it. buy it. do it.

How much		money? time? coffee?	**How many**	dollars/ francs/yen? minutes? cups of coffee?	He's	taller older poorer	than she is.
					She's	shorter younger richer	than he is.

70

Now test yourself!

1 **Read the ten questions. What are the answers to nine of the questions?**

1 What does Bernard do? ☐

2 What's he doing? ☐

3 When does he finish? ☐

4 When is he going to finish? ☐

5 What does Susan do? ☐

6 What is she doing? ☐

7 Does she smoke? ☐

8 Is she smoking? ☐

9 What do you do? ☐

10 What are you doing? ☐

A I'm not sure but I don't think so.
B This exercise.
C She's a journalist.
D He's an art expert.
E Usually at six or at six thirty.
F He's working.
G No, she isn't. Look. Can't you see?
H Soon.
I She's talking to someone.

There is no answer here for one question.

Write the number here. ☐

2 **Which word is wrong?**

1 blue green (new) red
2 wife son mother daughter
3 father brother son daughter
4 child man boy girl
5 single married man wife
6 see eye look ear
7 ear hear listen eye
8 talk nose speak mouth
9 people children men woman

3 **What is the word?**

1 You drink it. It has no colour.
water

2 You eat it. Cheese, meat, bread, eggs are examples of it. **f**_____

3 Teachers do this when students don't understand something. **ex**_____

4 It is a picture but you take it with a camera. **ph**_____

5 A man or a woman. **p**_____

6 Very young people. **ch**_____

4 **Write the questions.**

1 I live in London. What about you? Where _do_ you _live?_

2 I work in London. Where _____ you _____ ?

3 I'm married. _____ you _____, too?

4 I've got two children. How _____ children _____ you _____ ?

5 I've got a brother and a sister. _____ you _____ a brother and a sister, too?

6 I'm going to see her tomorrow. _____ you _____ to see your sister, too?

7 I'm sitting near a window now. _____ you _____ near a window, too?

8 I can see a street and a lot of people. What _____ you _____

31 Thursday morning

It's eight o'clock in the morning. The weather isn't very good this morning.

Bernard can see a lot of dark clouds. He thinks it is going to rain. He often walks to work. If it rains, he is going to take a taxi.

Diana Brentano and Larry Jasper are in London. She is looking at a photograph. She is going to cut Larry's hair. Then she is going to do some other things to his hair and face.

1 Answer the questions.

1 Is it raining?
2 What is Bernard going to do if it rains?
3 What is Diana doing?
4 What is she going to do?

It is ten thirty now. Bernard is talking to some students. He is going to finish in a few minutes. When he finishes, he is going to have a cup of tea. After that, he is going to talk to a journalist.

Larry is going to look into the mirror. When he does that he is going to see a big difference.

2 Answer these questions.

1 Who is Bernard talking to?
2 Who is he going to talk to when he finishes?
3 What is Larry going to see when he looks into the mirror?
4 Look at Larry in picture two and in picture four. What is the difference?

Vocabulary

3 **Look.**

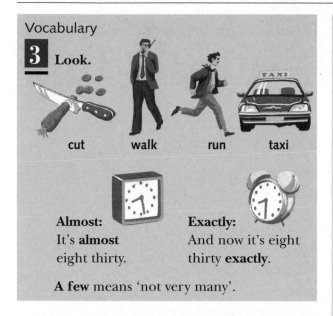

cut   walk   run   taxi

Almost:
It's **almost**
eight thirty.

Exactly:
And now it's eight
thirty **exactly**.

A few means 'not very many'.

Pronunciation

4 **Say these words with your teacher.**

A	B
thirty	thirteen
moment	because
Friday	enough

5 **Say these words, too. Nine of them have the same stress as thirty. Which three have the same stress as thirteen?**

prob-lem, mor-ning, fin-ish, be-gin,
Sun-day, Mon-day, Tues-day, to-day,
weath-er, stu-dent, af-ter, be-fore

🖭 **Now listen. Are you right?**

6 **Now write the nine words with the same stress as thirty. Then write the three words with the stress of thirteen.**

thirty

1 problem   6 ....
2 ....   7 ....
3 ....   8 ....
4 ....   9 ....
5 ....

thirteen

1 begin
2 ....
3 ....

Grammar

7 **Read these sentences. In two and three, Susan is sure she going to see Bernard.**

If I see Bernard tomorrow, I want to ask him some questions.

When I see Bernard tomorrow, I want to ask him some questions.

When I see him, I'm going to ask him some questions.

If I see him, I'm going to ask him some questions.

Two sentences here mean "Perhaps I'm going to see Bernard. I'm not sure". Which two? Say them.

8 **Complete the sentences with 'if' or 'when'.**

1 What are you going to do tomorrow
   _____if_____ the weather is good?

2 I'd like to go shopping tomorrow
   .... the weather is bad.

3 But .... the weather is good,
   I'd like to walk in the park.

4 What does the teacher usually say
   .... the lesson finishes?

5 The teacher usually says "That's all for
   now. Goodbye." .... the
   lesson finishes.

6 What are you going to do ....
   the lesson finishes?

9 **What about you? Answer the questions.**

1 What would you like to do next Sunday if
   the weather is good?

2 What would you like to do next Sunday if
   it rains?

Classic Extra page 109

32

Are you afraid?

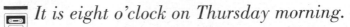 *It is eight o'clock on Thursday morning.*

LARRY	We have to do it today.
TONY	Today?
LARRY	Yes. Today.
TONY	But... I need more time. You have to give me more time.
LARRY	I can't give you any more time.
TONY	But... but...
LARRY	What's wrong? Are you afraid?
TONY	No, I'm not afraid. But I'm worried.
LARRY	Why are you worried?
TONY	What if something goes wrong?
LARRY	Nothing is going to go wrong.
TONY	But what if... what if...
LARRY	I don't want to hear that again.
TONY	What?
LARRY	I don't want to hear "What if...". I don't want to hear "But". I have to do it today. You have to help me. And you're going to help me!

1 What do you think?
Give these answers to the questions.

> *I think so.*   *I don't know.*
>
> *I don't think so.*   *I'm not sure.*
>
> *I think they're going to...*

1 What are they going to do today?
2 Do you think it's something good?
3 Do you think it's something bad?
4 Does Tony want to do it?
5 Why is he worried?

2 Listen to more of the conversation.
Then answer the questions.

1 Who do you think Larry and Tony are talking about?
2 What does that person always do on Thursday?
3 What does he or she usually do?
4 Look at this picture. Does it help you to understand something Larry says? If it helps you, explain to someone else what Larry says.

Vocabulary

3 **Look.**

1 **Have to:** If you **have to** do something tomorrow, it is necessary for you to do it: "You have to give me more time."

2 **Need:** When something is necessary and you haven't got it, you can say you **need** it: "Tony needs money."

3 **Help:** When you do something for someone or give them something, you **help** them: "I need money. Can you help me?"

4 **Nothing** is the opposite of **something**:
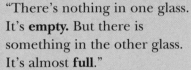
"There's nothing in one glass. It's **empty.** But there is something in the other glass. It's almost **full.**"

5 **Again:** When you do something more than once, you do it **again**: "I like the film. I'm going to see it again."

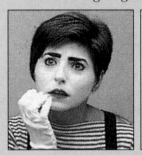

worried   afraid

Pronunciation

4 Say the words. Is the stress the same as <u>thir</u>ty or is it the same as thir<u>teen</u>?

1 nothing	6 afraid
2 question	7 shopping
3 explain	8 picture
4 something	9 again
5 worried	

 Now listen. Are you right?
Now ⟨circle⟩ six words the same as <u>thir</u>ty.
Tick (✓) three words the same
as thir<u>teen</u>.

Grammar

5 **Look. It is necessary for Susan to do these things today.**

She **has to**	do some shopping. buy an umbrella. write some letters.

And this is what she is thinking now.

I **have to**	do some shopping. buy an umbrella. write some letters.

6 **What about you? Answer the questions.**

1 Do you need something today or tomorrow? Do you have to buy or get something? What?

2 Do you have to go somewhere? Where?

3 What about the day after tomorrow? What do you have to buy? Where do you have to go? What do you have to do?

4 What do you have to do next week? Who do you have to see? Where do you have to go?

7 **Ask other people questions with 'what' and 'when'.**

What do you have to do next week?	*go to...* *I have to buy...* *see...*
When do you have to...	*On...* *At...*

8 **Now write sentences about yourself.**

I have to ....
.... tomorrow.
I have to ....
.... the day after tomorrow.
I have to ....
on ....

Classic Extra page 109

33

A strange question

🔲 *Susan Farr is a journalist.*

SUSAN   I'm very interested in this picture. And I'd like more information about the artist. I don't know very much about him.

BERNARD   His name was Bruno Sharp.

SUSAN   When was he born? And where?

BERNARD   He was born in... excuse me, but...

SUSAN   Yes?

BERNARD   Do I know you?

SUSAN   No, I don't think so.

BERNARD   I know it's a strange question but your face is familiar. Wait, I remember now. Were you in London on Saturday? On a bus?

SUSAN   Yes, I was.

BERNARD   You asked me some questions.

SUSAN   Yes, of course. I remember now, too. Your wallet was on the seat next to you.

1 Right or wrong?

1 Susan wants some information about Bruno Sharp.
2 Bruno Sharp was an artist.
3 Bernard doesn't know anything about Bruno Sharp.
4 He can remember Susan's face.
5 Susan is on a bus now.
6 She was on a bus and Bernard was on the same bus.
7 His wallet is on the seat next to her.
8 His wallet was on the seat next to him.

2 What about you?

1 Look at the person next to you. Is that face familiar?
2 Do you know that person?
3 What do you know about him or her?
4 Were you born in 1901?
5 Where were you born?
6 Were you in London yesterday?
7 Were you on a bus last Sunday?
8 Where is your wallet now?
9 What is in it?

Vocabulary

3 Look.

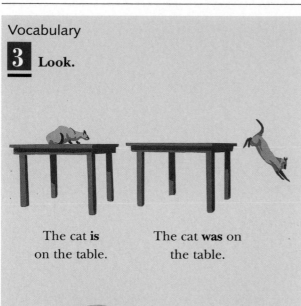

The cat **is**   The cat **was** on
on the table.   the table.

He **was born**   He **died**   This is
in 1901.   in 1974.   an **artist**.

1 **Familiar:** Someone or something you
   think you know is **familiar**.
2 **Strange** means 'not familiar'.
3 **Of course:** We say this when we are very
   sure the answer is 'Yes': "Do you love
   me?" - "Yes, of course."

Pronunciation

4 Listen to these words. Six of them have
the same stress as <u>yes</u>-ter-day. Three
have same stress as re-<u>mem</u>-ber.

pho-to-graph, to-mor-row, Sat-ur-day,
beau-ti-ful, cin-e-ma, ex-pen-sive,
fam-i-ly, ter-ri-ble, mu-se-um

**Now circle the three words with the
same stress as re-<u>mem</u>-ber.**

Grammar

5 Look.

Present: | I | am | here | now.

Past:

I He She It	was	here in London	yesterday. last week. last month. last year.
We You They	were	here in London	

6 **What's the next word?**

I am, She is, We...   *are*

1 I am, She is, He...
2 I was, He was, You...
3 We were, They were, It...
4 We are, He is, They...
5 They were, It was, I...

7 **How many questions can you ask other
people? What are the answers?**

yesterday?

Where were you   *at six o'clock*
                   at seven o'clock   *the day before
                   at eight o'clock*   *yesterday?*
                   at nine o'clock

                   last   *Monday?
                            Tuesday?
                            Wednesday?*

I can't remember.

I was in...

I'm not sure, but I think I was in...

Classic Extra page 110

77

34

The Woman with Green Eyes

This is a picture in the Gibson Museum of Art in Oxford. It is called 'The Woman with Green Eyes'. It is in Bernard Winter's office.

The artist's name is on the picture. He finished the picture in 1974.
Bruno Sharp was born in Amsterdam in 1901. He died in England in 1974. He lived in Holland, the United States and in Switzerland. He was not a very happy man. His life was sad but very interesting.

The face you see in the picture is his wife's face. Her name was Verena. People said she was very beautiful. She died in New York in 1939. It was winter. It was very cold.

There is another picture called 'Summer in the Park' in the museum in Oxford. Bruno Sharp painted it, too.

1 Answer the questions.

1 Where is this picture now?
2 What is it called?
3 Why is it called that?
4 When did Bruno Sharp finish it?
5 When and where was he born?
6 When and where did he die?
7 Who was this woman in the picture?
8 When and where did she die?
9 Bruno Sharp painted a lot of pictures. Can you give the name of one more?

2 Listen and answer the questions.

1 How many people are talking?
2 Who are they?
3 Where are they?
4 Where are they going now?
5 What time is it?

Vocabulary

 Look.

| to paint | happy | sad |

1 **Summer:** The time of year when it is very warm.
2 **Winter:** The time of year when it is very cold.
3 **Life:** The time from when you are born to when you die. "I am reading a book about the life of Albert Einstein."
4 **Interesting:** Something is **interesting** if you are interested in it. If you say "That person is very interesting", it means "I want to know about him or her".

4 **Perhaps you don't know some of these words. But what is the wrong word?**

1 last week yesterday 1901 (tomorrow)
2 Monday April Thursday Friday
3 winter spring summer month
4 day autumn week year
5 picture book photograph painting
6 warm sun winter summer

Pronunciation

5 **Say the words. In which word is the sound different?**

1 lived, give, (life,) women
2 life, light, wife, winter
3 you, beautiful, museum, your
4 summer, nothing, other, museum
5 want, warm, door, daughter, walk

🔲 **Now listen. Are you right?**

Grammar

6 **Look.**

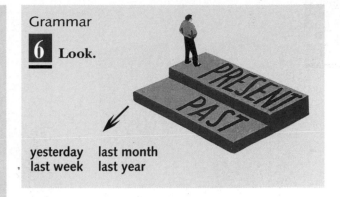

yesterday last month
last week last year

7 **Say these sentences. Are they present or past?**

It's cold. → Present.
It was cold. → Past.

1 It's warm.
2 It was warm.
3 Bernard lives in Oxford.
4 Bruno Sharp lived in Zurich.
5 Bernard and Susan were on a bus.
6 Larry and Diana are in London.
7 I finished work at six.
8 We finish work at five thirty.

8 **Complete the sentences with 'was', 'were', 'is', 'am', 'finishes' or 'finished'.**

1 The weather _is_ not very good today.
2 Susan _____ in London yesterday.
3 She and Bernard _____ on the same bus last Sunday.
4 Bernard usually _____ work at six.
5 Yesterday he _____ at seven.
6 I _____ not very interested in modern art.

9 **Write three sentences about yourself.**

I was born in _____.
I live in _____ now.
In 1994, I lived in _____.

Classic Extra page 110

35

What about lunch?

🔊 *Susan and Bernard are talking*

SUSAN Tell me more about Bruno Sharp.

BERNARD He was born in Amsterdam, but he went to New York in nineteen thirty-two. He lived and worked there for fifteen years. Then, in nineteen forty-seven, he went to Zurich. He finished this picture there. It was his last picture.

SUSAN His last picture. Oh, do you mean...

BERNARD Yes, it's a sad story. Very sad.

SUSAN I'd like to hear it.

BERNARD All right, but it's almost lunch time. Are you hungry?

SUSAN Am I hungry?

BERNARD Yes, I mean, would you like to have lunch with me?

SUSAN Oh, that would be very nice. Thank you.

1 Right or wrong?

1 Bruno Sharp lived and worked all his life in Amsterdam.
2 After he finished 'The Woman with Green Eyes', he finished many more pictures.
3 Susan doesn't want to hear any more about Bruno Sharp.
4 She is going to have lunch with Bernard.

2 What about you?

1 Are you hungry?
2 What do you usually have for lunch?
3 When do you usually have lunch?
4 Do you know what you are going to have for lunch tomorrow?
5 What would you like to have for lunch tomorrow?
6 Where did you have lunch yesterday?

Vocabulary

3 Look.

1 **To tell** someone something means you say something to them: "Say 'Hello' to Harry and tell him that I am well."

2 **A story** has a beginning, a middle and an end: "Mothers often tell their children stories before they go to bed."

3 **Hungry:** When you want or need food, you are **hungry**.

4 **Almost** means not exact but near: "It's almost three o'clock."

5 **Every:** If you do something **every** day, you do it seven days a week: "I get up every morning at the same time."

4 Read these sentences. Does 'have' mean 'eat', 'drink' or 'have'?

1 Can I have a cup of tea, please? *Drink.*

2 Can I have your telephone number? *Have.*

3 I usually have a cheese sandwich for lunch. *Eat.*

4 I always have a cup of coffee in the morning.

5 I have a reservation for three nights.

6 Do you often have tea in the morning?

7 I never have spaghetti in the morning.

8 You have got a very good accent.

Pronunciation

5 You can hear the same sound again and again in these sentences. What is it?

I'd like t<u>o</u> tell you <u>a</u> little <u>a</u>bout Bernard Winter. He w<u>a</u>s born <u>i</u>n Manchester <u>a</u>nd went t<u>o</u> school there. When he w<u>a</u>s twenty-three, he went t<u>o</u> London <u>a</u>nd now he's <u>a</u>n art expert. You c<u>a</u>n read more <u>a</u>bout him on the next page.

Now listen. Are you right?

Grammar

6 Look.

These verbs are regular.

Present	Past
finish/finishes	finish**ed**
like/likes	lik**ed**
work/works	work**ed**

Why do we call these verbs irregular?

Present	Past
go/goes	went
do/does	did
see/sees	saw
come/comes	came
have/has	had
drink/drinks	drank

7 Say 'past' or 'present'.

 I go to work. *Present.*

I went to work. *Past.*

1 He watches television every day.
2 He watched television every day.
3 They had lunch at one.
4 They have lunch at one.
5 Bruno Sharp lived in New York.
6 Bruno Sharp lives in New York.
7 I buy a newspaper in the morning.
8 I bought a newspaper in the morning.

Which of the eight examples are regular and which are irregular?

8 Talk and write about yourself.

I usually have lunch at _____.

Yesterday, I had lunch at _____.

I often go to _____

on Saturday.

Last Saturday I went to _____.

I often drink _____ in the evening.

Yesterday evening I drank _____.

Classic Extra page 111

36

📼 *Bernard and Susan are having lunch.*

SUSAN   I don't eat meat very often. I prefer fish. But the lamb is delicious.

BERNARD   Yes, I had it last week. It was excellent.

SUSAN   How is the chicken?

BERNARD   Oh, it's... it's...

SUSAN   Yes?

BERNARD   Oh, I'm thirsty.

SUSAN   Thirsty? Would you like some water?

BERNARD   Yes. Where's the waiter?

SUSAN   He's coming now.

BERNARD   Oh dear...

SUSAN   What's wrong?

BERNARD   I'm very sorry, but... I think...

SUSAN   Yes?

BERNARD   I think I'm ill.

SUSAN   Ill? Do you need a doctor?

Do you need a doctor?

1 **Answer the questions.**

1 What is Susan eating?
2 Does she eat it very often?
3 What is Bernard eating?
4 What did he eat in the restaurant last week?
5 What's wrong?

2 **What about you?**

1 How often do you eat meat? Every day? Often? Not very often? Never?
2 How often do you eat fish?
3 Which do you prefer in the morning, coffee or tea?
4 How often do you need a doctor?
5 What do you usually do when you are ill?

3 📼 **Bernard and Susan are talking before they eat. Listen. Then answer the questions.**

1 What do you think the waiter means when he says "Can I have your order?"
   • How are you going to pay?
   • Where would you like to go?
   • What would you like to eat?
2 What would Susan like?
3 What is the problem?
4 What are they going to drink?

Vocabulary

 Say the right answer.

1 If you **prefer** something, you...
- don't like it.
- like it more than another thing.
- like it but don't like other things.

2 If you say "The food was **delicious**", you mean...
- I liked it very much.
- It wasn't bad but it wasn't very good.

3 **Excellent** means...
- very, very good.
- good but not very good.

4 If you say "I'm **thirsty**", you want...
- food.   • sleep.   • water.

5 If you say "I'm **ill**", you mean...
- I'm very well.
- I'm not well.

6 When people are very ill, they need...
- a waiter.   • a doctor.

7 A good answer to "How is the chicken?" is...
- It's very well.   • It's very good.

5 **What's the wrong word?**

1 food   fish   (television)   bread
2 fish   meat   money   cheese
3 meat   bread   lamb   chicken
4 doctor   hotel   ill   hospital
5 lunch   music   dinner   breakfast
6 am   are   was   is

Pronunciation

 Say the words. In which word is the sound different?

1 <u>b</u>ottle, num<u>b</u>er, hus<u>b</u>and, (lam<u>b</u>)
2 <u>b</u>orn, w<u>or</u>d, w<u>or</u>k, thi<u>r</u>sty
3 <u>sh</u>e, informa<u>t</u>ion, deli<u>c</u>ious, fu<u>t</u>ure
4 <u>ch</u>eap, pic<u>t</u>ure, <u>ch</u>ampagne, fu<u>t</u>ure
5 <u>s</u>trange, <u>g</u>et, <u>d</u>angerous, <u>G</u>eorge

 Now listen. Are you right?

Grammar

7 **Look at the two questions.**

| Susan | **is** | in Oxford today. |
| **Is** | Susan | in Oxford today? |

| Susan | **was** | in Oxford yesterday, too. |
| **Was** | Susan | in Oxford yesterday, too? |

8 **Ask questions about the past.**

1 The weather is good today.
<u>Was</u> it good yesterday?

2 Larry is in Oxford today.
_____ he in Oxford yesterday, too?

3 There are a lot of people here today.
_____ there a lot of people yesterday?

4 Are you ill?
_____ you ill yesterday?

5 Five men are here today.
How many men _____ here yesterday?

9 **Which questions are about the past?**

1 Do you need a doctor?
2 Did you need a doctor?
3 Did you like it?
4 Do you like it?

10 **You need the same word in all of these questions about the past. What is it?**

1 Where _____ you go yesterday?

2 What _____ you do yesterday?

3 What _____ you have for lunch yesterday?

4 Where _____ you have lunch yesterday?

5 _____ you drink a lot of wine yesterday?

Ask other people the same questions.

Classic Extra page 111

37

What happened yesterday?

📼 *Bernard had lunch with Susan yesterday.*

The food was very good. They liked it but Bernard ate very little. He drank a little wine and then he was very ill. He almost died.

A few minutes later, a man went into Bernard's office. There was a picture there. The man came out of Bernard's office a few minutes later. Bernard's secretary saw him. "I thought he was Bernard. He looked exactly like him", she said later. She went into Bernard's office. The picture wasn't there.

At two fifteen in the afternoon, Larry Jasper went to a big house near Oxford. He had something with him. Another man wanted it. The other man gave Larry a lot of money for it. At three o'clock, Larry came out of the house. Two detectives stopped him.

1 **Answer the questions.**

1 What happened when Bernard had lunch?
2 What happened a few minutes later?
3 What happened at two fifteen?
4 What happened at three o'clock?

2 **What do you think?**

1 A man went into Bernard's office at one forty-five. Who was that man?
2 What did he want?
3 Why did the other man give Larry money?

3 **What about you?**

1 Where were you yesterday afternoon?
2 What did you do?
3 Who did you see?

Vocabulary

4 Look.

 What **happened** yesterday?

This question means "What did you do? What did you see? What did you hear? What did other people do?"

a little wine   **a few** glasses of wine

"**A little** wine" means 'not much wine'. We use 'a little' with words like 'wine, water, coffee' and 'money'. "**A few** glasses of wine" means 'not many'. We use 'a few' with words like 'glasses of wine, cups of coffee, dollars, people, books' etc.

5 Many words in English have different meanings. Look at these examples. Does the underlined word mean the same thing? Or is the meaning different?

1 Basil <u>had</u> champagne and fish for lunch. Basil <u>had</u> more hair when he was younger. *Different.*

2 Do you <u>like</u> this kind of food? English food isn't <u>like</u> Italian food.

3 Is the weather in England <u>like</u> the weather in your country? Does Bernard look <u>like</u> Larry?

4 They <u>looked</u> at the menu and then ordered. Diana <u>looked</u> out of the window.

5 Maureen <u>looked</u> at the man. "He <u>looked</u> like Bernard," she said later.

Grammar

6 Look at the present and past forms of these verbs. Some past forms are not here. What are those past forms?

Present	Past
work/works	worked
want/wants	
like/likes	
finish/finishes	
go/goes	went
see/sees	
give/gives	gave
drink/drinks	
need/needs	needed
do/does	
buy/buys	bought
eat/eats	ate

7 Now say you did these things yesterday.

Are you going to London tomorrow?

No, I went to London yesterday.

1 Are you going to see your friends today? No, I .... them yesterday.

2 Are you going to do that exercise on page 83 today? No, ... it ....

3 Are you going to have lunch in that new restaurant tomorrow? No, I .... lunch there yesterday.

4 Are you going to buy a new car today? No, I .... a new car yesterday.

8 How many things can you say and write about yourself?

Yesterday	needed a...
Last week	wanted to buy...
Last month	saw a...
Last year	bought a...

Classic Extra page 112

38

How strange

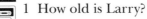

Bernard Winter was very ill yesterday.

SUSAN   How are you today, Bernard?

BERNARD Much better. What's the weather like?

SUSAN   The same as yesterday. Did you read the newspaper this morning?

BERNARD Yes, I did. That man walked into my office and stole that picture. And my secretary saw him. Why didn't she stop him?

SUSAN   Because she thought he was you.

BERNARD What? How strange.

SUSAN   It's much stranger than you think. I've got some more information about the man. You're going to be very surprised when I tell you about him.

1 Answer the questions.

1 How is Bernard today?
2 What's the weather like there today?
3 What did Larry Jasper do yesterday?
4 Why didn't Bernard's secretary stop him?
5 What is Susan going to do?

2 What about you?

1 How are you today?
2 How were you yesterday?
3 What's the weather like today?
4 What was it like yesterday?
5 How was your lunch yesterday?

3 Listen to Susan talking about Larry.

1 How old is Larry?
2 When was he born?
3 Where was he born?
4 What was his mother's name?
5 How old was Bernard when his mother died?
6 Why is Susan surprised?

Vocabulary

 Say the right answer.

1 When people ask "How are you today?", a good answer is...

- Very well, thank you. How are you?
- Very good. Are you good, too?

2 When people want to know about the weather, they usually ask...

- How is it?
- What's it like?

3 If the weather was terrible yesterday but today you can see a little sun, you can say the weather is...

- worse than it was.
- better than it was.

4 If people **steal** something, they...

- pay for something and take it.
- take something but do not pay for it.

5 The woman in this photo looks...

- worried.
- surprised.
- sad.

Pronunciation

 In which word is the sound different?

1 st<u>ea</u>l, s<u>ee</u>, p<u>eo</u>ple, (<u>better</u>)
2 s<u>aw</u>, th<u>ough</u>t, b<u>ough</u>t, en<u>ough</u>
3 st<u>o</u>le, g<u>o</u>, n<u>ow</u>, kn<u>ow</u>
4 str<u>a</u>nge, inform<u>a</u>tion, secret<u>a</u>ry, d<u>ay</u>

Now listen. Then say all the words with these sounds:

1 'ea' in st<u>ea</u>l   3 'o' in st<u>o</u>le
2 'aw' in s<u>aw</u>   4 'ay' in d<u>ay</u>

Grammar

 Look at these infinitives with 'to'.

It's going **to rain** today.
I have **to work** late this evening.

The infinitive is also in questions and negative sentences with no 'to'.

Did you **see** it? I don't **understand**.
What do you **mean**?
I didn't **know** that.

Now look at these examples.

Present	Past	Infinitive
work/works	worked	to work
go/goes	went	to come
like/likes	liked	to like
do/does	did	to do
watch/watches	watched	to watch
buy/buys	bought	to buy

7 Say the infinitive forms.

	Present	Past	Infinitive
1	want/wants	wanted	to _want_
2	see/sees	saw	to _____
3	need/needs	needed	to _____
4	think/thinks	thought	to _____
5	tell/tells	told	to _____
6	has/have	had	to _____

8 Complete the sentences.

1 I had fish for lunch yesterday. What _did_ you _have_ for lunch yesterday?

2 I did a lot of work yesterday. What about you? What _____ you _____ yesterday?

3 Last Saturday I went to the cinema, saw a film and then had a drink in a pub. What about you? _____ you _____ to the cinema? _____ you _____ a film? _____ you _____ a drink in a pub?

Classic Extra page 112

39 I didn't know

🔲 *Two detectives are talking to a waiter.*

TONY	I didn't do it.
JACK	Yes, you did! You put something in his wine. Something dangerous.
TONY	I didn't know. I didn't know.
SHIRLEY	You didn't know? What didn't you know?
TONY	I didn't know it was dangerous. Larry Jasper gave it to me. But he didn't tell me.
JACK	What do you mean?
TONY	He didn't tell me that it was dangerous.
JACK	So you put something in Bernard Winter's wine.
TONY	Yes, but I didn't know it was dangerous.
JACK	But Bernard Winter almost died after he drank it! That's why he's in hospital. So it was dangerous.
TONY	How is he?
SHIRLEY	He's better today. He was much worse yesterday.
TONY	I didn't know. I didn't know.

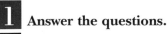

1 Answer the questions.

1 Where is Bernard today?
2 How is he?
3 Why was he ill yesterday?
4 What didn't Tony know?
5 Why didn't he know?

2 Listen to more of the conversation. Then say which sentences are right and which are wrong.

1 Tony knows Basil and his daughter.
2 He knows Basil's daughter but not Basil.
3 He knew that Basil gave Larry fifty thousand.
4 The detectives knew but Tony didn't know.
5 Larry gave Tony a lot of money, too.

Vocabulary

3 **Say the right answer.**

1 A **hospital** is a place people go to when they are...
   • very hungry.   • very thirsty.   • very ill.
2 Bernard was very ill yesterday but is not very ill today.
   Today he is...
   • better.   • worse.   • the same.
3 Which of these animals do you think is very **dangerous?**
   • A dog.   • A cat.   • A tiger.

a tiger

Grammar

4 **Look at these negative sentences in the past.**

He	did		He		do	
She	liked		She		like	
I	knew		I		know	
You	wanted	it.	You	didn't	want	it.
We	had		We		have	
They	saw		They		see	

5 **Now say the negative forms.**

1 He went.   He ___didn't___ go.

2 They came.   They didn't _____ .

3 I saw it.   I _____ it.

4 We worked.   We _____ .

5 I watched it. I _____ it.

6 I bought it. I _____ it.

6 **Complete these sentences.**

1 I liked it. You ___didn't___ like it.

2 You knew it. I didn't _____ it.

3 You saw Larry, but I _____ see him.

4 I gave it to you. You _____
   it to me.

5 You drank the wine. I _____ drink it.

6 This happened but that
   didn't _____ .

7 **Bernard did these things yesterday. Did you do them, too? Talk to someone.**

I had lunch.
I had a glass
  of wine.
I was very ill.
I went to
  hospital.
I almost died.

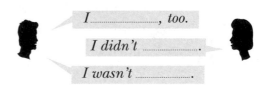

I _____ , too.

I didn't _____ .

I wasn't _____ .

8 **One of you says the word on the left. The other says the opposite on the right.**

cold	forget
present	finish
summer	warm
better	boring
strange	well
expensive	short
remember	winter
ill	familiar
a lot	a little
start	past
tall	worse
interesting	cheap

Classic Extra page 113

40

Why didn't he tell me?

Susan is talking to Bernard in hospital.

SUSAN So you didn't know your mother?

BERNARD No, I didn't. I knew her name. That's all.

SUSAN Is it possible that you have a twin brother?

BERNARD I don't think so.

SUSAN Why not?

BERNARD Because my father never told me.

SUSAN Yes, but think about it, Bernard. Larry looks like you. You and he were born on the same day, in the same place, in the same year. His mother died at the same time that your mother died. Perhaps his mother was your mother, too.

BERNARD But... but if that's true, why didn't my father tell me? It isn't possible. I can't believe it.

SUSAN Almost everything is possible, Bernard. Journalists know that.

1 Answer the questions.

1 Why can't Bernard believe he has a twin brother?
2 Why does Susan think it is possible?
3 What did Bernard know about his mother?

2 Ask other people questions.

1 Was someone near you now born on the same day but not in the same year?
2 Was someone near you now born in the same place?

3 Listen and answer the questions.

1 Two people are talking. Who are they?
2 What did one of the people read this morning?
3 One of these people has got some information. Do you think Bernard would like to have this information, too?
4 What is that information?
5 Why didn't Bernard know this?

Vocabulary

 Say the right answers.

1 When something is **possible**...
  • it happened or can happen.
  • it didn't happen or it can't happen.

2 If you have a **twin** brother or sister, you and your twin have the same mother...
  • but you were born on different days.
  • and you were born on the same day.

3 The word **place** means...
  • a city, a country, a house, a street where you are or were yesterday.
  • a person or a number of people.

4 Which sentence do you think is **true**? Which sentence is not true, or **false**?
  • London is a very small city.
  • London is a very big city.

5 If I say something and you think it is true, you...
  • believe me.   • don't believe me.

6 If you can believe **everything** I say, you...
  • believe a lot of things I say but not all of them.
  • believe all the things I say.

Grammar

 Which word in each sentence tells you that the sentence is about the past?

1 My father never told me.
2 Did he tell you?
3 Why didn't he tell you?

6 **Complete these sentences.**

1 Did you __work__ late on Thursday?

2 Basil gave Larry a lot of money. Why _____ he _____ him a lot of money?

3 Larry didn't _____ Tony a lot of money. Why _____ he _____ him more money?

4 Bernard didn't work yesterday. Why _____ he _____ yesterday?

Pronunciation

 In which word is the sound different?

1 <u>k</u>ind, li<u>k</u>e, thin<u>k</u>, loo<u>k</u>, (<u>k</u>new)
2 kn<u>ow</u>, n<u>ow</u>, t<u>o</u>ld, g<u>o</u>
3 po<u>ss</u>ible, diffi<u>c</u>ult, se<u>c</u>re<u>t</u>ary, <u>t</u>able
4 bel<u>ie</u>ve, <u>s</u>ee, d<u>ie</u>, <u>e</u>vening, p<u>e</u>ople
5 tr<u>ue</u>, f<u>oo</u>d, g<u>oo</u>d, <u>wh</u>o, tw<u>o</u>,
6 <u>wh</u>at, <u>qu</u>estion, <u>Qu</u>een, <u>wr</u>ite

🔲 **Now listen. Are you right?**

8 **Larry did these things yesterday. These things happened to him. Did people in your class do them, too? Did they happen to them, too? Ask questions.**

1 He went to a museum.
2 He was in his car.
3 He stole a picture.
4 He saw Basil Newton.
5 Basil gave him a lot of money.
6 Two detectives stopped him.

Did you go to a museum yesterday?

Yes, I did.

No, I didn't.

9 **What three things did you do yesterday? Did other people in your class do them, too? Ask questions.**

Classic Extra page 113

Progress Check 4 — Units 31-40

If I see Bernard tomorrow, I'm going to ask him some questions.
> = Perhaps I'm going to see Bernard.

When I see Bernard tomorrow, I'm going to ask him some questions.
> = I'm sure I'm going to see Bernard.

I'd We'd	like	to go to the cinema this evening. to watch television this evening. to listen to some music this evening.

Questions

Would	you	like	to go to the cinema this evening? to watch television this afternoon? to listen to some music this morning?

'd = would.

He She	has to	work late tomorrow. go to London next week.

I You We/They	have to	see a doctor now. do it now. go now.

Questions

Does	he she	have to	work late tomorrow? go to London next week?

Do	I you we/they	have to	see a doctor now? do it now? go now?

Have to = It is necessary. Perhaps you don't want to do it but you **have to** do it.

I/He/She/It You/We/They	was were	in London here	yesterday. the day before yesterday.

Was/were = The past form of 'be'.

I/He/She It We/You They	lived... worked... needed... finished...

Regular verbs in the past end in -d or -ed.

I/He/She/It We/You/They	went/saw... did/bought...

These are irregular verbs in the past.

Questions

Did	you/he/she/we/they	work/go/need/see/do/finish/buy...?

Negatives

I/She/He/It/We/You/They	didn't	work/go/need/see/do/finish/buy..

Use 'did/didn't' for regular and irregular questions and negatives in the past.

Now test yourself!

1 **What are the answers? Write A–G**

1 Where were you yesterday evening? [D]
2 What did you have? ☐
3 How was it? ☐
4 Would you like a cup of tea? ☐
5 Do you like tea? ☐
6 What do you do? ☐
7 What did you do yesterday? ☐

A I went to work, came home, watched
   television and then went to bed.
B Yes, please. Thank you very much.
C I work in an office.
D In that new Italian restaurant.
E Yes, but I prefer coffee.
F Very good.
G I can't remember the word. I think it
   was 'linguini' or something like that.

2 **Circle the word which is wrong.**

1 thirsty (hungry) water drink
2 hungry waiter restaurant hospital
3 came had know drank
4 dangerous afraid worried happy
5 clouds weather food rain

3 **Write negative sentences.**

1 Larry is a nice man.
  Larry _isn't_ a nice man.
2 Bernard lives in London.
  Bernard _____ live in London.
3 He worked late yesterday.
  He _____ _____ late yesterday.
4 It's going to rain today.
  It _____ _____
  _____
5 I knew that.
  I _____ _____ that.

4 **Write the questions.**

1 Bernard was ill yesterday. What
  about you? _Were_ _____ you _ill_
  yesterday?
2 Susan likes fish. What about you?
  _____ you _____ fish?
3 She saw Bernard yesterday. _____ you
  _____ Bernard yesterday?
4 She is going to see him tomorrow.
  _____ you _____
  _____ him tomorrow?
5 She'd like to go to Paris. _____ you
  _____ _____ _____ to Paris?
6 She was born in Canada.
  Where _____ you born?
7 She lived in Toronto when she was
  younger. Where _____ you _____
  when you _____ younger?
8 She has to do a lot of things tomorrow.
  What _____ you _____ to do?

5 **What is the word?**

1 It is a bird. Bernard ate it for
  lunch and then he was ill. **ch**_icken_
2 People go there when they are very ill.
  h_____
3 You can say someone's face is this if you
  think you know that person. **f**_____
4 This word means "to like something
  more than another thing". **to p**_____
5 The opposite of 'remember'. **f**_____
6 The opposite of 'better'. **w**_____

Classic Extra

Unit 1

1 Write the words.

| Bernard | Hello | My | my | name's |
| name's | name | Susan | What's | your |

Hello, ... Susan.
What's .... ?

.... Bernard.

2 Write the numbers in words.

3 _three_   1 ....   8 ....   7 ....   2 ....

4 ....   5 ....   9 ....   6 ....   3 ....

Unit 2

1 Write the words.

in in in ~~near~~ near or

1 Is New York _near_ San Francisco?

2 Is Oxford .... Ireland?

3 What time is it .... San Francisco?

4 Is Boston .... New York?

5 Is London a big .... a small city?

6 Is Boston .... America?

Answer the questions 1–6.

☐ Yes.   ☐ It's big.   ☐1 No.
☐ It's one o'clock.   ☐ Yes.   ☐ No.

2 Write the numbers in words.

17 _seventeen_   10 ....   15 ....

20 ....   13 ....   18 ....

11 ....   19 ....   12 ....

3 Write the words.

1 in London is America
London is in America.

2 England is Manchester in
Manchester

3 small London a is city
....

4 a city New York big is
....

5 Ireland big a country is
....

6 Scotland is Oxford in
....

Now look at 1–6. Write 'yes' or 'no'.

1 _No._   3 ....   5 ....

2 _Yes._   4 ....   6 ....

Unit 3

1 **Write the questions.**

1 What is _____ the Green Parrot?   It's a café.

2 _____ _____ the Green Parrot?   It's in London.

3 _____ the Green Parrot a _____ café?   No, it's a small café.

2 **Now write these questions.**

1 What _____ _____ it?   It's eight o'clock.

2 _____ _____ Dublin?   It's in Ireland.

3 _____ _____ Boston?   It's near New York.

4 _____ _____ your telephone number?   It's 01937 698421.

5 _____ _____ Manchester?   It's a city.

3 **Write the numbers in words.**

22 _____   30 _____   34 _____   58 _____

40 _____   46 _____   50 _____   60 _____

Unit 4

1 **Write the words.**

| are   are   Boston   from   from   from   in   I'm |
| Is   near   Pardon   ~~Where~~   Yes   York   you   you |

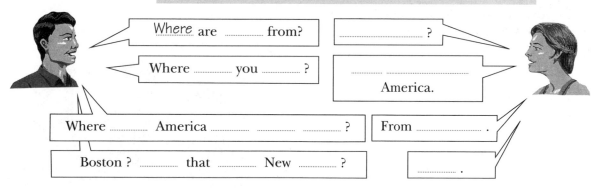

Where are _____ from?

_____ ?

Where _____ you _____ ?

_____ America.

Where _____ America _____ _____ ?

From _____ .

Boston ? _____ that _____ New _____ ?

_____ .

2 **Answer the questions.**

1 Where's Diana from? (Manley) She's from Manley.

2 Where's Larry from? (Liverpool) He's from _____

3 Where's Susan from? (Toronto) _____

4 Where are Larry and Diana now? (London) _____

5 Where's Bernard from? (Manchester) _____

Classic Extra

Unit 5

1 How much is it?
Write the questions. Write the answers in words.

1 How much is a _glass_ of wine? ....

2 How much is a .... of tea? ....

3 How much is a
   cheese .... ? ....

4 How much is a .... of water? ....

2 Complete the sentences.

1 A man from England is _English._   5 A man from Italy is ....

2 A Canadian woman is from _Canada._   6 A man from Germany is ....

3 A woman from Japan is ....   7 A Spanish woman is from ....

4 A French woman is from ....   8 A man from America is ....

3 Write these numbers in words.

200 ....   83 ....   92 ....

101 ....   100 ....   74 ....

Unit 6

1 Write the questions. 'How many?'
or 'how much?'

1 _How many men are there_ ? Two.

2 _How much are the_
  newspapers ? 30p.

3 .... ? Three.

4 .... ? Four.

5 .... ? Six.

6 ....
  .... ? £1.75.

2 What time is it?

1 **19.00** _Seven o'clock in the evening._   3 **14.15** ....

2 **9.30** ....   4 **18.30** ....

Unit 7

1 **There are seven sentences. What are they?**

1 The Queen
2 St. James's Park
3 There are
4 There are
5 There are
6 Harrods
7 Victoria Station

[ ] a lot of
[ ] a lot of trees
[ ] is one of
[ ] isn't far
[ ] is
[1] lives
[ ] seven million people in

[ ] department stores in London.
[ ] a department store.
[ ] from Waterloo Station.
[ ] four big parks in London.
[ ] in the park.
[ ] London.
[1] near Victoria Station.

2 **What is it? What are they? Write sentences.**

1 London is a city.

2 The Thames

3 Victoria and Waterloo

4 Selfridges and Harrods are

Unit 8

1 **Write the sentences about Larry and Diana.**

| are | ~~he~~ | he | her | his | ~~is~~ | is | is | lives | lives | she | she | she | they |

1 He is from Liverpool.

2 _____ from Australia.

3 _____ in London now.

4 _____ Australian.

5 _____ near Victoria Station.

6 _____ in a flat in London now.

7 _____ last name is Jasper.

8 _____ last name is Brentano.

2 **Write the questions.**

1 Shirley Jack are and where Where are Shirley and Jack ? In an office.

2 the where office is _____ ? In London.

3 tired Shirley is _____ ? Yes.

4 is man the photograph who the in _____ ? Larry.

5 the in woman the who photograph is

_____ ? Diana.

6 last what names their are _____ ? Jasper and Brentano.

7 is Larry from where _____ ? Liverpool.

8 and Diana where now are Larry _____ ? In London.

Unit 9

1 Write the sentences.

> Behind this bus. ~~Excuse me.~~ Is this the bus to Oxford Circus?
> No, that's the bus there. Thank you. The seventy-three?
> Where? ~~Yes?~~ Yes, that's right.

A <u>Excuse me.</u>   B ....

B <u>Yes?</u>   A ....

A ....   B ....

B ....   A ....

A ....

2 Complete the sentences with these words.

> ~~her~~ his his her my their their your

1 <u>Her</u> name's Diana.

2 .... name's Bernard.

3 .... names are Bernard and Susan.

4 .... name's Larry.

5 "What's .... name?" - "My name's Diana."

6 "What's your name?" - "............ name's Larry.'

7 .... names are Diana and Larry.

8 .... name's Shirley.

Unit 10

1 Write the sentences with 'is', 'isn't', 'are' or 'aren't'.

1 Marble Arch <u>isn't</u> in Liverpool.

2 Larry and Diana .... American.

3 Bernard and Susan .... on a bus.

4 Larry .... from Australia.

5 Susan and Bernard .... in Liverpool now.

6 The fourth stop .... after the third stop.

2 Write the words. You are at Victoria now.

> Victoria ⇨ Hyde Park ⇨ Marble Arch ⇨ Edgeware Road ⇨ Paddington

1 Hyde Park is the <u>next</u> stop.

2 Paddington is the <u>third</u> stop after Hyde Park.

3 Marble Arch is the .... stop after Hyde Park.

4 What's the .... stop? Hyde Park.

5 Marble Arch is the stop .... Edgeware Road.

6 Edgeware Road is the .... stop after Hyde Park.

7 Paddington is the stop .... Edgeware Road.

Unit 11

1 **Write the sentences.**

1 a Larry flat in lives   Larry lives in a flat.

2 Bernard London in lives

3 Street lives in Rutland Diana

4 London Street in Rutland is

5 Station lives Paddington Diana near

Are the sentences 1–5 right (✓) or wrong (✗)?   1 ✔   2 ....   3 ....   4 ....   5 ....

2 **What is the opposite? Write 1– 8.**

1 big	2 good	3 first	4 here	5 left	6 man	7 near	8 right
☐ bad	☐ far	☐ last	☐ right	1 small	☐ there	☐ woman	☐ wrong

Unit 12

1 **Answer the questions.**

1 Does Larry live in Oxford?   No , he lives in London.

2 Does Larry live in a house?   No ,

3 Is Larry's flat in Rutland Street?   No , it's

4 Is his flat on the first floor?   No ,

5 Are all the windows closed now?   No , one

6 Is the window on the right open?   ,

2 **What can you see from your window? Write the questions and answer 'yes, I can' or 'no, I can't'.**

1 Can you see a _park_ ?

2 Can you see a .... ?

3 Can you see a .... ?

Unit 13

1 Write sentences about Diana.

1 + big cities   _She likes big cities._

2 - English weather   _She doesn't_

3 - English men

4 + London

5 - classical music

6 + coffee

7 + fish

2 Write six things you can eat and five things you can drink.

~~abder~~	~~eebr~~	ceeehs	aet	ceeffo	aertw	firtu
	einw	fhis	aemt	acdhinsw		

You can eat: _bread_   f

           _c_   _m_

           _f_   a _s_

You can drink: _beer_   t

           _c_   _w_

           _w_

Unit 14

1 Write the questions.

1 where/work   _Where do you work?_   I work in an office.

2 where/live   I live in Oxford.

3 like/Oxford   Yes, it's a very old city.

4 live/house   No, I live in a flat.

5 interested in art   Yes, but not in modern art.

6 interested in books   Yes, I like books.

2 Look at the the woman in Exercise 1. Write sentences about her.

1 She _____ in an office.   4 She _____ in a flat.

2 She _____ in Oxford.   5 She _____ in modern art.

3 She _____ Oxford.   6 She _____ in books.

3 What is the opposite? Write 1–7.

1 buy	2 old	3 last	4 terrible	5 there	6 in front of	7 small
☐ here	☐ 1 sell	☐ nice	☐ big	☐ new	☐ first	☐ behind

Unit 15

1 **What is the first word of these questions? 'Do' or 'does'?**

1 I live in London.   <u>Do</u> you like London?

2 She lives in London.   .... she like London?

3 He lives in London.   .... he like London?

4 We live in London.   .... you like London?

5 They live in London.   .... they like London?

2 **Write the questions. No names, please!**

1 Diana/work in films   <u>Does she work in films?</u>

2 Diana and Larry/live in London

3 Larry/sell cheap cars

4 Martin/like his job

5 Pat and Olga/work in an office

6 Susan/live in New York

7 Diana/like wine

Unit 16

1 **Write the questions.**

1 Larry live does where   <u>Where does Larry live?</u>

2 does in living what Larry do his room

3 Larry where shower take a does

4 where breakfast eat Larry does

5 many in rooms Larry's how there flat are

6 does for breakfast eat Larry what

7 is flat where Larry's

2 **Now answer the questions in Exercise 1 with these words.**

1 (flat)   <u>He lives in a flat.</u>

2 (television)

3 (bathroom)

4 (kitchen)

5 (four)

6 (toast)

7 (London)

Classic Extra

Unit 17

1 **Write about the man, woman or people.**

1 _She can see_ _____

2 _They_ _____

3 _He_ _____

2 **Complete the sentences with these words.**

can	can't	car	cup	doesn't	doors	eats	flat	hear	~~is~~	is
is	kitchen	morning	reads	room	street	toast	which			

Jack 1 _is_ in Larry's 2 _____ in London. Shirley 3 _____ in a 4 _____ in the 5 _____ .

Jack can 6 _____ Shirley, but he 7 _____ see her. Jack 8 _____ in Larry's

9 _____ . This is where Larry 10 _____ breakfast (a 11 _____ of coffee and

12 _____) and 13 _____ the newspaper in the 14 _____ . Jack 15 _____ see

four 16 _____ in the flat. But 17 _____ door is the door to the living 18 _____ ? Jack

19 _____ know.

Unit 18

1 **Write the words.**

~~always~~	never	often	sometimes	usually

Number of days a week:	4	0	7	2	6
	_____	_____	_always_	_____	_____

2 **Write about Cathy. She works with Bernard, in the museum in Oxford.**

1 drink tea in the morning (7 days a week)
2 eat breakfast in her kitchen (6 days)
3 go to a café for lunch (4 days)
4 watch television in the evening (2 days)

1 _She always drinks tea in the morning._

2 _____

3 _____

4 _____

3 **Write questions about Tom with 'where', 'what' or 'when'. Tom works with Bernard, too.**

1 _Where does he work?_ _____ He works in a <u>museum</u>.

2 _____ He starts work at <u>nine o'clock</u>.

3 _____ He goes <u>to a café</u> for lunch.

4 _____ He finishes work at <u>six o'clock</u>.

Unit 19

1 **Write the words.**

| always | because | can't | closed | closed | go |
| is | it | it's | Monday | museum | Yes |

We .... to the .... now, ... it's .... Why .... closed?

Because .... Is it .... on Monday?

....

Write sentences about Larry, Bernard and Diana.

1 Larry/live/Oxford (-) /London (+) Larry doesn't live in Oxford, he lives in London.

2 Larry/live/house (-) /flat (+)

3 Bernard/work/café (-) /museum (+)

4 Diana/like/tea (-) /coffee (+)

And now you!

5 I/like/... (-) /but ... (+) I don't like

Unit 20

Write the sentences.

1 on train Susan a is Susan

2 accent Susan got an has American

3 Canada is Susan from

4 Susan man is American thinks the

Are the sentences 1–4 right (✓) or wrong (✗)? 1 .... 2 .... 3 .... 4 ....

2 **Write about Larry and Susan. No names, please!**

1 She's got a .... cat.

2 .... pen.

3 .... bike.

4 .... camera.

5 .... watch.

And now you! Write 'yes, I have' or 'no, I haven't'.

6 Have you got a dog? ....

7 Have you got a car? ....

8 Have you got a house? ....

9 Have you got a flat? ....

Classic Extra

Unit 21

Who are these people in the family? Write the words.

1 nos   _son_   4 aefhrt   7 abdhnsu

2 ehmort   5 efiw   8 eirsst

3 adeghrtu   6 cdhil   9 cdehilnr

Complete these sentences.

1 " _Have_ you _got_ a daughter?" - "Yes, I _have_ ." - "What's _her_ name?"

2 "............ Susan .... a sister?" - "Yes, she ...." - "What's .... name?"

3 "............ Laura and Bill .... a daughter?" - "Yes, they ...." - "What's .... name?"

4 "............ Bill .... a brother?" - "Yes, he ...." - "What's .... name?"

5 "We .... two children." - "Oh! What .... names?"

6 "Robert .... two sisters." - "Oh! What .... names?"

7 "............ Sonia .... a son?" - "Yes, she ...." - "What's .... name?"

8 "............ Frank and Sonia .... a son?" - "Yes, they ...." - "What's .... name?"

Unit 22

Write the questions. Write 'much' or 'many' in your questions.

1 sisters how you got (much/many) have   _How many sisters have you got?_

2 drink tea (much/many) how you do

3 he money (much/many) want does how

4 do work you hours (much/many) how

5 how you (much/many) time got have

6 how can see (many/much) you people

Write the second word of these pairs.

sell	house	question	son	hours	right
b _uy_	f	a	d	m	w

Write these numbers in words.

83,000   _eighty-three thousand_   20,000

15,000   42,000

Unit 23

1 Write these words.

eyes	hair	person
big		big

big   blue   dark   fair
fat   grey   long
tall   thin   short

2 Write these sentences with a '.

1 Tony loves the daughter of Basil. _Tony loves Basil's daughter._

2 She has got big blue eyes.

3 The wife of Harry works in a museum.

4 "I am not fat", he says.

5 Tony has not got a wife.

3 What's the opposite?

1 big _small_   3 long   5 fat   7 rich

2 tall   4 fair   6 ugly   8 single

Unit 24

1 What are the people doing?

1 _She's eating a sandwich._

2

3

4

5

6 _I'm_

2 Complete these sentences with 'this', 'that', 'these' or 'those'.

1 _That_ is my car there.   5 _____ is my bus here.

2 _____ are my newspapers here.   6 _____ is my sister there.

3 _____ are my books there.   7 _____ are my children there.

4 _____ is my house there.   8 _____ are my sandwiches here.

Classic Extra

Unit 25

Complete these sentences with 'someone' or 'something'.

1 " _Someone_ is coming." - "Who?"

2 "She's drinking _____." - "What?"

3 "He's showing her _____." - "What?"

4 "_____ is in the car." - "Who?"

Complete the pairs of words.

1 Two cars - One _car_

2 Two men - One _____

3 Two people - One _____

4 Two women - One _____

5 Two children - One _____

6 Two cities - One _____

Write the first word of these questions.

1 _Are_ Diana and Larry drinking coffee?

2 _Does_ Diana live in London?

3 _____ Diana and Larry eating in the restaurant?

4 _____ Larry smoking in the restaurant?

5 _____ Larry showing her a book?

6 _____ Larry smoke?

7 _____ Diana and Larry live in the same flat?

8 _____ Larry showing Shirley the photograph?

Unit 26

Complete these sentences.

1 Look _at_ this photograph.

2 I'm interested _____ that man.

3 Your hair is longer _____ his hair.

4 His eyes are the same colour _____ your eyes.

5 "How _____ is he?"- "Forty."

6 I'm not _____ how old he is.

7 "Are you younger than him?" - "I don't _____ . Perhaps I am, perhaps I'm not."

30 years,
1 metre 65

47 years,
1 metre 60

Write the sentences.

1 lot he (young) her is than a   _He is a lot younger than her._

2 than her he (tall) is   _____

3 lot is (old) she him than a   _____

4 is (short) him she little a than   _____

Unit 27

1 **Find the pairs.**

1 behind	2 late	3 yesterday	4 before	5 cheap	6 buy
☐ sell	☐ expensive	☐ early	☐ in front	☐ after	☐ tomorrow

2 **Complete the sentences.**

1 He never eats lunch. So, he _isn't going to eat lunch_ tomorrow.

2 She always starts at eight. So, she _is going to start at eight_ tomorrow.

3 They never work late. So, they _____ tomorrow.

4 He always finishes work at six. So, he _____ tomorrow.

5 They always watch TV after dinner. So, they _____ tomorrow.

6 He always buys a newspaper. So, he _____ tomorrow.

7 They never drink wine. So, they _____ tomorrow.

Unit 28

1 **Write the questions.**

1 evening Maureen this work to is going late
Is Maureen going to work late this evening?

2 Bernard late work is going evening to this
_____

3 talk going Bernard some is to students to tomorrow
_____

4 going time see is what to the Bernard students
_____

5 time speak journalist to the Bernard what to going is
_____

Answer the questions 1–5.

1 _No._ 2 _____ 3 _____ 4 _____ 5 _____

2 **Now look at your sentences in Unit 27 Exercise 2 on this page. Write the questions.**

1 _Is he going to have lunch tomorrow?_

2 _____

3 _____

4 _____

5 _____

6 _____

7 _____

Unit 29

What's the opposite?

1 remember _forget_

2 young ....

3 past ....

4 always ....

5 late ....

6 easy ....

Write these words from the past to the future.

1 _yesterday_ ....

2 ....

3 ....

4 ....

5 ....

6 ....

7 _next year_

> now   tomorrow evening
> this evening   ~~yesterday~~   ~~next year~~
> the day after tomorrow   next week

Complete the sentences with 'at', 'on' or ✗ (no word).

1 Larry is going to see __✗__ Susan Farr.

2 Bernard starts work .... nine o'clock.

3 What are you going to do .... Sunday?

4 Basil is going to give .... Larry £25,000.

5 Is Larry going to get the picture .... the day after tomorrow?

6 Is Bernard going to work .... Saturday?

Unit 30

Write the questions.

1 Susan reservation got a has   _Has Susan got a reservation?_

2 room has a double Susan got   ....

3 three Susan to going for nights is stay   ....

4 card Susan has a got credit   ....

5 newspaper to have a would like Susan   ....

6 shower got room a a with Susan has   ....

Write the questions with 'would like' and with no names!

1 John hasn't got a car.   _Would he like to have a car?_

2 Anna doesn't work in a museum.   ....

3 John and Anna don't live in a house.   ....

4 John hasn't got a lot of money.   ....

5 John and Anna don't finish work before seven.   ....

Unit 31

1 **Complete these sentences with 'every day', 'now', 'tomorrow' or 'yesterday'.**

1 He talked to her ....

2 He talks to her ....

3 He is going to talk to her ....

4 He is talking to her ....

2 **This is Anna speaking. Is she sure or not sure about these things?**

1 "I'm going to buy a new car when I have enough money."
   Is she sure she's going to have enough money?   ✔ Yes   ☐ No

2 "I'm going to write those letters if I have enough time."
   Is she sure she's going to have enough time?   ☐ Yes   ☐ No

3 "I'm going to give my mother this book when I see her next week."
   Is she sure she's going to see her mother next week?   ☐ Yes   ☐ No

4 "I'm going to see that film when my sister comes next week."
   Is she sure her sister is going to come next week?   ☐ Yes   ☐ No

5 "I'm going to work tomorrow if the weather is bad."
   Is she sure the weather is going to be bad tomorrow?   ☐ Yes   ☐ No

Unit 32

1 **Write the sentences.**

1 something he buy to has tomorrow   He has to buy something tomorrow.

2 she to tomorrow see has someone   ....

3 tomorrow help to have someone they   ....

4 read tomorrow she something to has   ....

5 have I something to tomorrow write   ....

Now write questions about sentences 1–5.

1 What does he have to buy?

2 ....

3 ....

4 ....

5 ....

2 **Complete the answers.**

1 Is she going to work tomorrow?   Yes, I _think_ so.

2 Can she speak French?   No, I .... think so.

3 Would he like to go there, too?   I .... know.

4 Have you got enough time?   I'm .... sure.

Unit 33

Complete the sentences with 'am', 'is', 'are', 'was' or 'were'.

Last week

1 I _was_ in London last week.

2 She _____ there last week.

3 We _____ at my brother's house last week.

4 They _____ in Oxford last week.

5 The weather _____ bad last week.

Today

6 I _____ in New York today.

7 She _____ here today.

8 We _____ at my sister's house today.

9 They _____ in London today.

10 The weather _____ good today.

Write the sentences.

1 is Bernard's Susan office in   Susan is in Bernard's office.

2 Sharp artist was Bruno an

3 in born he 1911 was

4 1974 died in he

5 knows Bruno Susan lot about a Sharp

6 bus Susan last on evening a Saturday was

7 seat Bernard's a on was next diary to him

Are sentences 1-7 right (✗) or wrong (✓)?

1 _____ 2 _____ 3 _____ 4 _____ 5 _____ 6 _____ 7 _____

Unit 34

What's the opposite?

1 happy   u_____

2 tomorrow   y_____

3 summer   w_____

4 warm   c_____

5 was born   d_____

6 something   n_____

Write the sentences.

Present

1 She lives in Oxford.

2 They are very happy.

3 _____

4 _____

5 It's cold.

6 He paints a lot of pictures.

Past

She lived in Oxford.

_____

Her eyes were green.

He finished work at six.

_____

_____

Unit 35

1 **Complete these sentences.**

1 They are _in_ his office.

2 They are talking .... the weather.

3 The photograph was .... the wall.

4 She was born .... New York.

5 She lived there .... twenty years.

6 He went .... New York in 1990.

7 They are interested .... music.

8 She's going to have lunch .... him.

9 I'd like a cup .... tea, please.

10 She always drinks tea .... the morning.

2 **Write 'every day' or 'yesterday' at the end of these sentences.**

1 I go to work _every day._

2 I went to work ....

3 I saw my sister ....

4 She comes here ....

5 They worked a lot ....

6 They had a problem ....

7 He drinks tea ....

8 They came to my house ....

Unit 36

1 **Write a word from A and a word from B to complete the sentences.**

(A) ~~hungry~~ good ill like more thirsty	(B) delicious doctor drink ~~eat~~ excellent prefer

1 If you are (A) _hungry_ , you need something to (B) _eat._

2 If you are (A) .... , you need something to (B) ....

3 If you are (A) .... , you need a (B) ....

4 If you (A) .... the food very much, you can say "It's (B) ....".

5 If you like fish (A) .... than you like meat, you can say "I (B) .... fish".

6 If the food is very, very (A) .... , you can say "It's (B) ....".

2 **Complete these questions about yesterday with 'did', 'was' or 'were'.**

1 Where _were_ they?

2 .... you go there, too?

3 What .... you eat?

4 What .... her problem?

5 .... your dinner good?

6 How many people .... there?

7 Why .... she see him?

8 Where .... their sons?

9 Why .... he ill?

10 .... the exercises difficult for you?

Unit 37

What is the past of these verbs?

are _were_   drink ....   go ....   see ....   come ....

eat ....   have ....   do ....   give ....   is ....

Complete these sentences with 'a few' or 'a little'.

1 There are only __a few__ people here.   4 I need .... more dollars.

2 I'd like .... wine, please.   5 I've only got .... money today.

3 I've only got .... English books.   6 She only works .... hours a week.

Complete the sentences with the verb in the past or in the future.

1 I (see) _saw_ my friends yesterday.   4 We (see) .... John next week.

2 She (have) .... lamb for dinner next Sunday.   5 We (have) .... lunch there last week.

3 He (eat) .... at six yesterday evening.   6 I (finish) .... this work tomorrow morning.

Unit 38

Write these sentences.

1 drank wine he his   He drank his wine.

2 buy is going he some to wine   ....

3 in he office an works   ....

4 the he watch is to news going   ....

5 restaurant her saw the in he   ....

6 going lunch him she with have is to   ....

7 money he lot gave a of him   ....

Are 1-7 in the past, present or future?   Past _1,_   Present ....   Future ....

Write the questions.

1 He gave her something yesterday.   What did he give her?

2 I saw someone yesterday.   Who ....

3 They bought something yesterday.   ....

4 I did something yesterday.   ....

5 She met someone in the evening.   Who ....

Unit 39

1 Write the verbs in the sentences. The first verb is always positive and the second verb is always negative. All the sentences are in the past.

buy	come
drink	eat
have	know
~~see~~	go

1 She _saw_ the film, but he _didn't see_ it.

2 She _____ the woman, but he _____ her.

3 She _____ a good day, but he _____ a good day.

4 She _____ a newspaper, but he _____ one.

5 She _____ here at six o'clock, but he _____ here.

6 She _____ lunch at The Green Parrot, but he _____ there.

7 She _____ red wine, but he _____ red wine.

8 She _____ to London, but he _____ with her.

2 What's the opposite of these words?

1 interesting b_____

2 strange f_____

3 winter s_____

4 better w_____

5 remember f_____

6 happy s_____

7 expensive c_____

8 yesterday t_____

Unit 40

1 Write the sentences.

1 thought was she he there   _She thought he was there._

2 mother he know his didn't   _____

3 at o'clock there went nine they   _____

4 him see London in they didn't   _____

5 didn't she Monday work on   _____

6 of he money gave lot her a   _____

7 up she at got six   _____

8 about he his told problem her   _____

2 Look at Exercise 1. Ask questions with 'Why...?'

1 _Why did she think he was there?_   5 _____

2 _Why didn't he know his mother?_   6 _____

3 _____   7 _____

4 _____   8 _____

Classic Extra Keys

Unit 1

Exercise 1

Hello, my name's Susan
What's your name?
My name's Bernard.

Exercise 2

3 three	1 one	8 eight
7 seven	2 two	4 four
5 five	9 nine	6 six
3 three		

Unit 2

Exercise 1

1 Is New York near San Francisco?
2 Is Oxford in Ireland?
3 What time is it in San Francisco?
4 Is Boston near New York?
5 Is London a big or small city?
6 Is Boston in America?

4 Yes.	5 It's big.
1 No.	3 It's one o'clock.
6 Yes.	2 No.

Exercise 2

17 seventeen	10 ten 15 fifteen
20 twenty	13 thirteen
18 eighteen	11 eleven
19 nineteen	12 twelve

Exercise 3

1 London is in America.
2 Manchester is in England.
3 London is a small city.
4 New York is a big city.
5 Ireland is a big country.
6 Oxford is in Scotland.

1 No.	3 No.	5 No.
2 Yes.	4 Yes.	6 No.

Unit 3

Exercise 1

1 What is the Green Parrot?
2 Where is the Green Parrot?
3 Is the Green Parrot a big café?

Exercise 2

1 What time is it?
2 Where is Dublin?
3 Where is Boston?
4 What is your telephone number?
5 What is Manchester?

Exercise 3

22 twenty-two	30 thirty
34 thirty-four	58 fifty-eight

40 forty	46 forty-six
50 fifty	60 sixty

Unit 4

Exercise 1

1 Where are you from?
2 Pardon?
3 Where are you from?
4 I'm from America.
5 Where in America are you from?
6 From Boston.
7 Boston? Is that near New York?
8 Yes.

Exercise 2

1 She's from Manley.
2 He's from Liverpool.
3 She's from Toronto.
4 They're in London.
5 He's from Manchester.

Unit 5

Exercise 1

1 How much is a glass of wine?
   One pound ninety.
2 How much is a cup of tea?
   Seventy pence.
3 How much is a cheese sandwich?
   One pound seventy-five.
4 How much is a bottle of water?
   Eighty pence.

Exercise 2

1 A man from England is English.
2 A Canadian woman is
   from Canada.
3 A woman from Japan is Japanese.
4 A French woman is from France.
5 A man from Italy is Italian.
6 A man from Germany is German.
7 A Spanish woman is from Spain.
8 A man from America is American.

Exercise 3

200	two hundred
83	eighty-three
92	ninety-two
101	one hundred and one
100	one hundred
74	seventy-four

Unit 6

Exercise 1

1 How many men are there?
   Two.
2 How much are the newspapers?
   30p.

3 How many women are there?
   Three.
4 How many cups are there?
   Four.
5 How many glasses are there?
   Six.
6 How much are the sandwiches?
   £1.75.

Exercise 2

1 19.00 Seven o'clock in
   the evening.
2 9.30 Nine thirty in the
   morning/Half past nine in
   the morning.
3 14.15 Two fifteen in the
   afternoon/Quarter past two in
   the afternoon.
4 18.30 Six thirty in the
   evening/Half past six in
   the evening.

Unit 7

Exercise 1

1 The Queen lives near
   Victoria Station.
2 St. James's Park is one of four big
   parks in London.
3 There are a lot of department
   stores in London.
4 There are a lot of trees in
   the park.
5 There are seven million people
   in London.
6 Harrods is a department store.
7 Victoria Station isn't far from
   Waterloo Station.

Exercise 2

1 London is a city.
2 The Thames is a river.
3 Victoria and Waterloo
   are stations.
4 Selfridges and Harrods are
   department stores.

Unit 8

Exercise 1

1 He is from Liverpool.
2 She is from Australia.
3 They are in London now.
4 She is Australian.
5 He lives near Victoria Station.
6 She lives in a flat in London now.
7 His last name is Jasper.
8 Her last name is Brentano.

Exercise 2
1 Where are Shirley and Jack?
2 Where is the office?
3 Is Shirley tired?
4 Who is the man in the photograph?
5 Who is the woman in the photograph?
6 What are their last names?
7 Where is Larry from?
8 Where are Larry and Diana now?

Unit 9
Exercise 1
A Excuse me.
B Yes?
A Is this the bus to Oxford Circus?
B No, that's the bus there.
A Where?
B Behind this bus.
A The seventy-three?
B Yes, that's right.
A Thank you.

Exercise 2
1 Her name's Diana.
2 His name's Bernard.
3 Their names are Bernard and Susan.
4 His name's Larry.
5 What's your name? My name's Diana.
6 What's your name? My name's Larry.
7 Their names are Diana and Larry.
8 Her name's Shirley.

Unit 10
Exercise 1
1 Marble Arch isn't in Liverpool.
2 Larry and Diana aren't American.
3 Bernard and Susan are on a bus.
4 Larry isn't from Australia.
5 Susan and Bernard aren't in Liverpool now.
6 The fourth stop is after the third stop.

Exercise 2
1 Hyde Park is the next stop.
2 Paddington is the third stop after Hyde Park.
3 Marble Arch is the first stop after Hyde Park.
4 What's the next stop? Hyde Park.
5 Marble Arch is the stop before Edgeware Road.
6 Edgeware Road is the second stop after Hyde Park.

7 Paddington is the stop after Edgeware Road.

Unit 11
Exercise 1
1 Larry lives in a flat.
2 Bernard lives in London.
3 Diana lives in Rutland Street.
4 Rutland Street is in London.
5 Diana lives near Paddington Station.

1 ✔	3 ✔	
2 ✗	4 ✔	5 ✔

Exercise 2
1 small   5 right
2 bad   6 woman
3 last   7 far
4 there   8 wrong

Unit 12
Exercise 1
1 No, he lives in London.
2 No, he lives in a flat.
3 No, it's in Green Parrot Street.
4 No, it's on the ground floor.
5 No, one of the windows is open.
6 No, the window on the left is open/on the right is closed.

Exercise 2
1 Can you see a park?
2 Can you see a house?
3 Can you see a church?

Unit 13
Exercise 1
1 She likes big cities.
2 She doesn't like the English weather.
3 She doesn't like English men.
4 She likes London.
5 She doesn't like classical music.
6 She likes coffee.
7 She likes fish.

Exercise 2
You can eat: bread fruit cheese meat fish a sandwich
You can drink: beer tea coffee wine water

Unit 14
Exercise 1
1 Where do you work?
2 Where do you live?
3 Do you like Oxford?
4 Do you live in a house?
5 Are you interested in art?
6 Are you interested in books?

Exercise 2
1 She works in an office.
2 She lives in Oxford.
3 She likes Oxford.
4 She lives in a flat.
5 She is not interested in modern art.
6 She is interested in books.

Exercise 3
1 sell   5 here
2 new   6 behind
3 first   7 big
4 nice

Unit 15
Exercise 1
1 Do you like London?
2 Does she like London?
3 Does he like London?
4 Do you like London?
5 Do they like London?

Exercise 2
1 Does she work in films?
2 Do they live in London?
3 Does he sell cheap cars?
4 Does he like his job?
5 Do they work in an office?
6 Does she live in New York?
7 Does she like wine?

Unit 16
Exercise 1
1 Where does Larry live?
2 What does Larry do in his living room?
3 Where does Larry take a shower?
4 Where does Larry eat breakfast?
5 How many rooms are there in Larry's flat?
6 What does Larry eat for breakfast?
7 Where is Larry's flat?

Exercise 2
1 He lives in a flat.
2 He watches television.
3 He takes a shower in the bathroom.
4 He eats breakfast in the kitchen.
5 There are four rooms in his flat.
6 He eats toast for breakfast.
7 His flat is /It's in London.

Unit 17
Exercise 1
1 She can see him.
2 They can see him.
3 He can't see her.

Exercise 2

1 is 2 flat 3 is 4 car
5 street 6 hear 7 can't 8 is
9 kitchen 10 eats 11 cup
12 toast 13 reads
14 morning 15 can 16 doors
17 which 18 room
19 doesn't

Unit 18

Exercise 1

4 - often
0 - never
7 - always
2 - sometimes
6 - usually

Exercise 2

1 She always drinks tea in
  the morning.
2 She usually eats breakfast in
  her kitchen.
3 She often goes to the café
  for lunch.
4 She sometimes watches television
  in the evening.

Exercise 3

1 Where does he work?
2 What time/When does he
  start work?
3 Where does he go for lunch?
4 What time/When does he
  finish work?

Unit 19

Exercise 1

We can't go to the museum now,
  because it's closed.
Why is it closed?
Because it's Monday.
Is it always closed on Monday?
Yes.

Exercise 2

1 Larry doesn't live in Oxford, he
  lives in London.
2 Larry doesn't live in a house, he
  lives in a flat.
3 Bernard doesn't work in a café,
  he works in a museum.
4 Diana doesn't like tea, she
  likes coffee.
5 (Example:) I don't like toast or
  coffee, but I like my flat and
  watching television.

Unit 20

Exercise 1

1 Susan is on a train.

2 Susan has got an American
  accent.
3 Susan is from Canada.
4 The man thinks Susan is
  American.

1 ✔ 2 ✗ 3 ✔ 4 ✔

Exercise 2

1 She's got a cat.
2 He's got a pen.
3 She's got a bike.
4 He's got a camera.
5 She's got a watch.

Unit 21

Exercise 1

1 son   6 child
2 mother   7 husband
3 daughter   8 sister
4 father   9 children
5 wife

Exercise 2

1 "Have you got a daughter?" - "Yes,
  I have." - " What's her name?"
2 "Has Susan got a sister?" - "Yes, she
  has." - "What's her name?"
3 "Have Laura and Bill got a
  daughter?" - "Yes, they have." -
  "What's her name?"
4 "Has Bill got a brother?" - "Yes, he
  has." - "What's his name?"
5 "We have got two children." -
  "Oh! What are their names?"
6 "Robert has got two sisters." -
  "Oh! What are their names?"
7 "Has Sonia got a son?" - "Yes, she
  has." - "What's his name?"
8 "Have Frank and Sonia got a son?"
  - "Yes, they have." -
  "What's his name?"

Unit 22

Exercise 1

1 How many sisters have you got?
2 How much tea do you drink?
3 How much money does he want?
4 How many hours do you work?
5 How much time have you got?
6 How many people can you see?

Exercise 2

buy flat answer daughter
minutes   wrong

Exercise 3

83,000 eighty-three thousand
20,000 twenty thousand
15,000 fifteen thousand
42,000 forty-two thousand

Unit 23

Exercise 1

eyes - big blue dark grey
hair - grey dark fair long short
person - big tall thin fat short

Exercise 2

1 Tony loves Basil's daughter.
2 She's got big blue eyes.
3 Harry's wife works in a museum.
4 "I'm not fat", he says.
5 Tony hasn't got a wife.

Exercise 3

1 small   5 thin
2 short   6 beautiful
3 short   7 poor
4 dark   8 married

Unit 24

Exercise 1

1 She's eating a sandwich
2 They're watching TV.
3 She's waiting for a bus.
4 He's drinking beer.
5 They're listening to music.
6 I'm...

Exercise 2

1 That is my car there.
2 These are my newspaper here.
3 Those are my books there.
4 That is my house there.
5 This is my bus here.
6 That is my sister there.
7 Those are my children there.
8 These are my sandwiches here.

Unit 25

Exercise 1

1 "Someone is coming." - "Who?"
2 "She's drinking something." -
  "What?"
3 "He's showing her something." -
  "What?"
4 "Someone is in the car." - "Who?"

Exercise 2

1 Two cars - One car
2 Two men - One man
3 Two people - One person
4 Two women - One woman
5 Two children - One child
6 Two cities - One city

Exercise 3

1 Are Diana and Larry
  drinking coffee?
2 Does Diana live in London?
3 Are Diana and Larry eating in
  the restaurant?

4 Is Larry smoking in the restaurant?
5 Is Larry showing her a book?
6 Does Larry smoke?
7 Do Diana and Larry live in the same flat?
8 Is Larry showing Shirley the photograph?

Unit 26

Exercise 1

1 Look at this photograph.
2 I'm interested in that man.
3 Your hair is longer than his hair.
4 His eyes are the same colour as your eyes.
5 "How old is he?" – "Forty."
6 I'm not sure how old he is.
7 "Are you younger than him?" – "I don't know. Perhaps I am, perhaps I'm not."

Exercise 2

1 He is a lot younger than her.
2 He is taller than her.
3 She is a lot older than him.
4 She is a little shorter than him.

Unit 27

Exercise 1

1 in front   4 after
2 early   5 expensive
3 tomorrow   6 sell

Exercise 2

1 So, he isn't going to eat lunch tomorrow.
2 So, she is going to start at eight tomorrow.
3 So, they aren't going to work late tomorrow.
4 So, he is going to finish work at six tomorrow.
5 So, they are going to watch TV tomorrow.
6 So, he is going to buy a newspaper tomorrow.
7 So, they aren't going to drink tomorrow.

Unit 28

Exercise 1

1 Is Maureen going to work late this evening?
2 Is Bernard going to work late this evening?
3 Is Bernard going to talk to students tomorrow?

4 What time is Bernard going to see the students?
5 What time is Bernard going to speak to the journalist?

1 No. 2 Yes. 3 Yes.
4 At 10 o'clock. 5 At 11 o'clock.

Exercise 2

1 Is he going to eat lunch tomorrow?
2 Is she going to start work at eight tomorrow?
3 Are they going to work late tomorrow?
4 Is he going to finish work at six tomorrow?
5 Are they going to watch TV tomorrow?
6 Is he going to buy a newspaper tomorrow?
7 Are they going to drink wine tomorrow?

Unit 29

Exercise 1

1 forget   3 future   5 early
2 old   4 never   6 difficult

Exercise 2

1 yesterday
2 now
3 this evening
4 tomorrow evening
5 the day after tomorrow
6 next week
7 next year

Exercise 3

1 Larry is going to see ✗ Susan Farr.
2 Bernard starts work at nine o'clock.
3 What are you going to do on Sunday?
4 Basil is going to give ✗ Larry £25,000.
5 Is Larry going to get the picture ✗ the day after tomorrow?
6 Is Bernard going to work on Saturday?

Unit 30

Exercise 1

1 Has Susan got a reservation?
2 Has Susan got a double room?
3 Is Susan going to stay for three nights?
4 Has Susan got a credit card?
5 Would Susan like to have a newspaper?

6 Has Susan got a room with a shower?

Exercise 2

1 Would he like to have a car?
2 Would she like to work in a museum?
3 Would they like to live in a house?
4 Would he like to have a lot of money?
5 Would they like to finish work before seven?

Unit 31

Exercise 1

1 He talked to her yesterday.
2 He talks to her every day.
3 He is going to talk to her tomorrow.
4 He is talking to her now.

Exercise 2

1 Yes   3 Yes   5 No
2 No   4 Yes

Unit 32

Exercise 1

1 He has to buy something tomorrow.
2 She has to see someone tomorrow.
3 They have to help someone tomorrow.
4 She has to read something tomorrow.
5 I have to write something tomorrow.

1 What does he have to buy?
2 Who does she have to see ?
3 Who do they have to help?
4 What does she have to read?
5 What do I have to write?

Exercise 2

1 Yes, I think so.
2 No, I don't think so.
3 I don't know.
4 I'm not sure.

Unit 33

Exercise 1

1 I was in London last week.
2 She was there last week.
3 We were at my brother's house last week.
4 They were in Oxford last week.
5 The weather was bad last week.
6 I am in New York today.
7 She is here today.

8 We are at my sister's house today.
9 They are in London today.
10 The weather is good today.

Exercise 2
1 Susan is in Bernard's office.
2 Bruno Sharp was an artist.
3 He was born in 1911.
4 He died in 1974.
5 Susan knows a lot about Bruno Sharp.
6 Susan was on a bus last Saturday evening.
7 Bernard's diary was on a seat next to him.
1 ✓ 2 ✓ 3 ✗ 4 ✓ 5 ✗ 6 ✓ 7 ✗

Unit 34

Exercise 1
1 unhappy   4 cold
2 yesterday   5 died
3 winter   6 nothing

Exercise 2
1 She lived in Oxford.
2 They were very happy.
3 Her eyes are green.
4 He finishes work at six.
5 It was cold.
6 He painted a lot of pictures.

Unit 35

Exercise 1
1 They are in his office.
2 They are talking about the weather.
3 The photograph was on the wall.
4 She was born in New York.
5 She lived there for twenty years.
6 He went to New York in 1990.
7 They are interested in music.
8 She's going to have lunch with him.
9 I'd like a cup of tea, please.
10 She always drinks tea in the morning.

Exercise 2
1 I go to work every day.
2 I went to work yesterday.
3 I saw my sister yesterday.
4 She comes here every day.
5 They worked a lot yesterday.
6 They had a problem yesterday.
7 He drinks tea every day.
8 They came to my house yesterday.

Unit 36

Exercise 1
1 If you are hungry, you need something to eat.

2 If you are thirsty, you need something to drink.
3 If you are ill, you need a doctor.
4 If you like the food very much, you can say "It's delicious".
5 If you like fish more than you like meat, you can say "I prefer fish".
6 If the food is very, very good, you can say "It's excellent".

Exercise 2
1 Where were they?
2 Did you go there too?
3 What did you eat?
4 What was her problem?
5 Was your dinner good?
6 How many people were there?
7 Why did she see him?
8 Where were their sons?
9 Why was he ill?
10 Were the excercises difficult for you?

Unit 37

Exercise 1
are - were	drink - drank
go - went	see - saw
come - came	eat - ate
have - had	do - did
give - gave	is - was

Exercise 2
1 There are only a few people here.
2 I'd like a little wine, please.
3 I've only got a few English books.
4 I need a few more dollars.
5 I've only got a little money today.
6 She only works a few hours a week.

Exercise 3
1 I saw my friends yesterday.
2 She is going to have lamb for dinner next Sunday.
3 He ate at six yesterday.
4 We are going to see John next week.
5 We had lunch there last week.
6 I am going to finish this work tomorrow morning.

Unit 38

Exercise 1
1 He drank his wine.
2 He is going to buy some wine.
3 He works in an office.
4 He is going to watch the news.
5 He saw her in the restaurant.
6 She is going to have lunch with him.
7 He gave him a lot of money.

Past 1, 5, 7   Present 3
Future 2, 4, 6

Exercise 2
1 What did he give her?
2 Who did you see?
3 What did they buy?
4 What did you do?
5 Who did she meet?

Unit 39

Exercise 1
1 She saw the film, but he didn't see it.
2 She knew the woman, but he didn't know her.
3 She had a good day, but he didn't have a good day.
4 She bought a newspaper, but he didn't buy one.
5 She came here at six o'clock, but he didn't come here.
6 She ate lunch at The Green Parrot, but he didn't eat there.
7 She drank red wine, but he didn't drink red wine.
8 She went to London, but he didn't go with her.

Exercise 2
1 boring   5 forget
2 familiar   6 sad
3 summer   7 cheap
4 worse   8 tomorrow

Unit 40

Exercise 1
1 She thought he was there.
2 He didn't know his mother.
3 They went there at nine o'clock.
4 They didn't see him in London.
5 She didn't work on Monday.
6 He gave her a lot of money.
7 She got up at six.
8 He told her about his problem.

Exercise 2
1 Why did she think he was there?
2 Why didn't he know his mother?
3 Why did they go there at nine o'clock?
4 Why didn't they see him in London?
5 Why didn't she work on Monday?
6 Why did he give her a lot of money?
7 Why did she get up at six?
8 Why did he tell her about his problem?

Progress Check 1 Units 1-10

1	2	3	4	5	6	7
1 C	1 Is	2 isn't	2 Her	2 men	2 There	2 is, Australia.
2 G	2 Are	3 aren't	3 their	3 women	3 There	3 is from Japan.
3 A	3 Is	4 I'm not	4 Our	4 glasses	4 It	4 is from Germany.
4 E	4 Are	5 aren't	5 Your	5 houses	5 There	5 is from Italy.
5 B	5 Are			6 shops	6 There	6 is from Spain.
6 D					7 It	
7 F						

Progress Check 2 Units 11-20

1	2	3	4	5
2 C	2 does	2 Can, see	2 doesn't buy, sell	2 it.
3 E	3 do	3 Does, like	3 doesn't like	3 them?
4 G	4 works	4 Do, go, on Saturday	4 aren't	4 him?
5 A	5 work	5 Does, watch, in the evening	5 don't like	5 her?
6 F	6 doesn't			
7 D	7 don't			

Progress Check 3 Units 21-30

1	2	3	4
1 D	2 son	2 food	2 do, work?
2 F	3 daughter	3 explain	3 Are, married
3 E	4 man	4 photograph	4 many, have, got?
4 H	5 man	5 person	5 Have, got
5 C	6 ear	6 children	6 Are, going
6 I	7 eye		7 Are, sitting
7 A	8 nose		8 can, see?
8 G	9 woman		
9 (There is no answer to this question.)			
10 B			

Progress Check 4 Units 31-40

1	2	3	4	5
2 G	2 hospital	2 doesn't	2 Do, like	2 hospital
3 F	3 know	3 didn't work	3 Did, see	3 familiar
4 B	4 happy	4 isn't going to rain today.	4 Are, going to see	4 to prefer
5 E	5 food	5 didn't know	5 Would, like to go	5 forget
6 C			6 were	6 worse
7 A			7 did, live, were	
			8 do, have	

Tapescripts for listening exercises

Unit 3 p10

Exercise 3

MAN	This is London. The time in London is now twelve oh five exactly.
WOMAN	This is Berlin. The time in Berlin is now one oh five and five seconds.
MAN	This is Moscow. The time in Moscow is now three oh five and ten seconds.
WOMAN	This is Tokyo. The time in Tokyo is now nine oh five and fifteen seconds.
MAN	This is Bangkok. The time in Bangkok is now eight oh five and twenty seconds.
WOMAN	This is Toronto. The time in Toronto is now seven oh one and twenty-five seconds.

Unit 5 p15

Exercise 7

WAITER	Yes?
WOMAN	How much is a cup of coffee?
WAITER	Ninety-five.
WOMAN	Ninety-five?
WOMAN	Yes. Ninety-five p.
MAN	Excuse me.
WAITER	Yes?
MAN	How much is a glass of wine?
WAITER	One sixty.
MAN	One pound sixty?
WAITER	Yes.
WOMAN	How much is a hamburger?
WAITER	Two fifty.
WOMAN	Two fifteen?
WAITER	No. Two fifty. Two five oh.
MAN	A cup of tea, please.
WAITER	Here you are. That's sixty p.
MAN	Sixty p? Here you are.

Unit 8 p20

Exercise 3

WOMAN	Where are you from, Bernard?
BERNARD	From Manchester.
WOMAN	Oh. Do you live there now?
BERNARD	No, I live in Oxford now.
WOMAN	Oh, I live in Oxford, too. Where in Oxford?
BERNARD	Pardon?
WOMAN	Where do you live in Oxford?
BERNARD	In Merton Street.

Unit 11 p28

Exercise 3

MAN	Where are you from, Susan?
SUSAN	Canada.
MAN	Canada? Oh. Where in Canada?
SUSAN	Toronto, but I don't live there now.
MAN	Oh? Where do you live?
SUSAN	In the United States. In New York. Here's my address.
MAN	One hundred and thirty Park Street, New York, New York. And is this your telephone number?
SUSAN	Yes. Nine nine seven, eight one one five.
MAN	Nine nine seven, eight one one five. Thank you.

Unit 13 p32

Exercise 3

MAN	Do you…
SUSAN	Yes?
MAN	Do you like London, Susan?
SUSAN	Well… it's very big and I don't like big cities. But…
MAN	Yes?
SUSAN	There are a lot of things I like here.
MAN	Oh? What?
SUSAN	I like the parks here. I like Hyde Park very much and Regent's Park, too. And the people. I like the people in London.
MAN	What about the food?
SUSAN	The food? Ah… the food. Hmm.
MAN	Yes, do you like the food?
SUSAN	Well, I like the cheese here.

The man laughs.

SUSAN	No, no! I think English cheese is very good! But I don't like the bread here.
MAN	What about fish and chips?
SUSAN	Fish and chips? English fish and chips?
MAN	Yes. What about English fish and chips? Do you like that?

SUSAN	I like fish very much, but I don't like English fish and chips. No.

Unit 15 p36

Exercise 3

SHIRLEY	Hello, Jack. Can you hear me? Jack? Where are you?
JACK	Hello, Shirley.
SHIRLEY	Where are you now?
JACK	I'm in Larry Jasper's flat. Where are you?
SHIRLEY	I'm in the car. Which room are you in, Jack? Which room are you in?
JACK	Hello?
SHIRLEY	Hello?
JACK	I'm in the…
SHIRLEY	What? Which room? Where?
JACK	I'm in the…
SHIRLEY	Pardon? I can't hear you. Jack? Jack?
JACK	Hello? Can you hear me? What's wrong with the radio?
SHIRLEY	I can't hear you, Jack. I can't hear you.
JACK	Hello?
SHIRLEY	Hello?

Unit 17 p40

Exercise 3

JACK	I'm in the living room now. I'm near the window.
SHIRLEY	What can you see?
JACK	A television, a chair and a table. Oh… I can see a photograph, too. It's on the table.
SHIRLEY	What can you see in the photograph?
JACK	Two people. One of them is a man and one of them is a woman. Ah… and there are two names on the photograph.
SHIRLEY	Can you see the two names?
JACK	Just a moment. Yes, I can see the names now.
SHIRLEY	What are the two names?
JACK	Uh… Maureen… Maureen Murphy and Ber… Ber…
SHIRLEY	Ber…? Ber… what?
JACK	Bernard. Bernard Winter.

Unit 19 p44

Exercise 2

DIANA	All right. It's…
LARRY	Yes?
DIANA	Oh one seven one…

LARRY	Just a moment. Oh one seven one…
DIANA	Two nine nine…
LARRY	Two double nine…
DIANA	One oh eight four.
LARRY	One oh eight four. Oh one seven one, two nine nine, one oh eight four.
DIANA	Yes.
LARRY	What's a good time to phone you?
DIANA	A good time? Not in the morning.
LARRY	So the morning is a bad time to phone you?
DIANA	Yes.
LARRY	What about the evening?
DIANA	Yes. I'm usually there in the evening.
LARRY	When in the evening?
DIANA	Nine or ten o'clock.
LARRY	Nine or ten o'clock in the evening. That's a good time to phone you. Right?
DIANA	Yes. That's right.

Unit 20 p46

Exercise 2

WOMAN	Sorry, What's your name?
TONY	Tony.
WOMAN	Tony… Tony what?
TONY	Stuart. Tony Stuart.
WOMAN	And where are you from, Tony?
TONY	From Bristol, but I live in Oxford now.
WOMAN	Oh? Do you like Oxford?
TONY	Yes, yes, I do. I like it very much.
WOMAN	Why?
TONY	Well it isn't a big city, but there are a lot of good things there. Good cinemas, good concerts, good restaurants…
WOMAN	Oh? Are there a lot of good restaurants in Oxford?
TONY	Well, not a lot, but there are some very good restaurants there. I work in one of them.
WOMAN	Oh, really?
TONY	Yes. I'm a waiter.

Unit 22 p52

Exercise 3

BASIL	I want your answer now, Larry.
LARRY	You can't have my answer now. Do you understand me, Basil? I want some time to think about it.
BASIL	All right, all right. When can you give me an answer?

LARRY	Four days from now.
BASIL	Four days from now. Today is Sunday. Tomorrow is Monday. The day after tomorrow is Tuesday. And the day after that is Wednesday.
LARRY	Yes, I know that, Basil.
BASIL	So I can have your answer on Wednesday. Is that right?
LARRY	That's right, Basil. You can have my answer on Wednesday.
BASIL	What time on Wednesday?
LARRY	What time is it now?
BASIL	Five thirty.
LARRY	You can have my answer exactly four days from now, at five thirty, on Wednesday.
BASIL	I've got a new telephone number. Here it is.
LARRY	Oh eight six, double three, double oh, double two. That's your new telephone number?
BASIL	Yes, that's my new telephone number. Oh eight six, double three, double oh, double two.

Unit 23 p 54

Exercise 2

BASIL	Well? Do you? Do you love him?
JULIET	I don't want to talk about him.
BASIL	But I want to talk about him. Now answer my question, Juliet.
JULIET	Why do you want to know?
BASIL	Because I'm your father, that's why. Do you love him?
JULIET	I like him very much.
BASIL	That isn't an answer to my question.
JULIET	No.
BASIL	No? What does that mean?
JULIET	No, I don't love him, daddy. But he loves me.
BASIL	Do you see him very often?
JULIET	No, not very often. He works in the evening.
BASIL	He works in the evening? What does he do?
JULIET	He's a waiter, daddy.
BASIL	A waiter!
JULIET	Yes, daddy. He's a waiter in a restaurant. He's a very nice boy. But I don't love him!

Unit 24 p 56

Exercise 3

JACK	Hello, Shirley.
SHIRLEY	Hello, Jack.
JACK	Where are you?
SHIRLEY	I'm in my car.
JACK	What are you doing?
SHIRLEY	I'm watching Larry Jasper.
JACK	Where is he?
SHIRLEY	He's in a car in front of me.
JACK	Can you see him?
SHIRLEY	Yes, I can see him
JACK	What's he doing?
SHIRLEY	He's talking. He's got a phone in his hand.
JACK	Where exactly are you?
SHIRLEY	In Rutland Street.
JACK	Rutland Street? Where's that?
SHIRLEY	Near Paddington Station.

Unit 26 p 60

Exercise 2

MAN	Have you got any brothers or sisters, Maureen?
MAUREEN	Yes. I've got one brother and one sister.
MAN	What are their names?
MAUREEN	Well, my brother's name is Patrick, and my sister's name is Bernadette.
MAN	How old are they?
MAUREEN	He's thirty-four. She's twenty-nine.
MAN	And can I ask you… how old are you?
MAUREEN	Thirty-one.
MAN	So Patrick is older than you are and Bernadette is younger.
MAUREEN	Yes.
MAN	Is Patrick very tall?
MAUREEN	No, I'm taller than he is. But he's taller than Bernadette.
MAN	Tell me a little more about Bernadette.
MAUREEN	Well, people say she's very beautiful. Her hair is the same colour as my hair.
MAN	So she's got fair hair, too?
MAUREEN	Yes. And green eyes.
MAN	Green eyes?
MAUREEN	Yes, Bernadette's got green eyes.

Unit 28 p 64

Exercise 3

DIANA	Hello?
LARRY	Hello, Diana. This is Larry.

DIANA	Why are you phoning so late?
LARRY	Late? Is it late?
DIANA	It's after eleven o'clock.
LARRY	I know. Listen. I want to see you tomorrow morning.
DIANA	Pardon?
LARRY	I want to see you tomorrow morning.
DIANA	Tomorrow morning?
LARRY	Yes.
DIANA	When? At what time?
LARRY	At eight o'clock.
DIANA	Eight in the morning?
LARRY	Yes. At eight. Understand?
DIANA	Where?
LARRY	There.
DIANA	Here? At my flat at eight?
LARRY	Yes. Have you got the make-up and the other things there?
DIANA	Yes. They're here.
LARRY	Good. See you tomorrow morning at eight. At your flat.
DIANA	Just a moment. Larry! Wait! Hello? Larry? Are you still there?

Unit 29 p66

Exercise 3

LARRY	I want twenty-five thousand before I get the picture. And I want twenty-five thousand after I get the picture. Do you understand?
BASIL	But... but that's fifty thousand.
LARRY	Do you want the picture or don't you?
BASIL	You know I want it.
LARRY	Well? Are you going to give me fifty thousand or aren't you?

* * *

	Are you there, Basil? Are you listening?
BASIL	Yes, I'm listening.
LARRY	Well, then. What's your answer?
BASIL	But it isn't going to be easy to get the money so...
LARRY	No 'buts'. I want twenty-five thousand before I get the picture, and then I want another twenty-five thousand after I get it. Do you understand that, Basil?
BASIL	All right. Twenty-five thousand before you get the picture for me, and twenty-five after you get it for me. But if you think you can...
LARRY	Goodbye, Basil. See you tomorrow.

Unit 30 p68

Exercise 3

SUSAN	What time is breakfast?
GIRL	From seven thirty to ten.
SUSAN	From seven thirty to ten. And where can I have it?
GIRL	In your room, or in our restaurant.
SUSAN	Where's the restaurant?
GIRL	It's on the first floor.
SUSAN	On the first floor. You mean, the floor above this one?
GIRL	Yes.
SUSAN	Sorry. I always forget that you call this the ground floor. It's the first floor in Canada.
GIRL	Oh, yes. Of course. Would you like to have breakfast in your room tomorrow morning or in the restaurant?
SUSAN	In the restaurant.
GIRL	Your room number is three thirteen. Here's your key.
SUSAN	Thank you.

Unit 32 p74

Exercise 2

LARRY	Nothing can go wrong. Now. Are you sure he's going to have lunch there?
TONY	Yes, I'm sure. He always has lunch in the restaurant on Thursday. And he always sits at the same table. It's reserved for him.
LARRY	What does he usually drink?
TONY	He usually has a glass of wine, but sometimes he drinks water.
LARRY	Hmm. What about coffee? Does he drink coffee, too?
TONY	Yes. He always has a cup of coffee at the end, when he finishes.
LARRY	I gave you a small bottle last Tuesday. Have you got it?
TONY	Yes, I've got it.
LARRY	If he orders wine, put three drops in his glass. But if he orders water, don't put anything in it. Wait. Then put three drops in his coffee. Do you understand?
TONY	Three drops if he orders wine. If he orders water, put three drops in his coffee. I understand. But listen, Larry.
LARRY	Yes?
TONY	What's in the bottle?
LARRY	Don't ask any more questions. Put three drops in his wine or in his coffee.

	Do you understand?
TONY	But… I want to know.
LARRY	What?
TONY	What's in that bottle? I mean, is it something… something d…
LARRY	Nothing is going to go wrong. Nothing.

Unit 34 p 78

Exercise 2

JACK	Where do you think he's going, Shirley?
SHIRLEY	I'm not sure, Jack. But this is the road to Oxford, isn't it?
JACK	Yes, this is the road to Oxford.
SHIRLEY	Well, Jack, perhaps he's going to Oxford.
JACK	That isn't Larry's usual car, is it?
SHIRLEY	No, it's different. It's a BMW. He usually drives a Mercedes. Oh, no!
JACK	What's wrong?
SHIRLEY	Look at the clock in this car. It says twelve fifty. Ten to one. That isn't the right time, is it?
JACK	No. My watch says twelve fifteen. And my watch is always right.
SHIRLEY	Yes. My watch says that, too. Twelve fifteen. A quarter past twelve.
JACK	You know, when Larry came out of that house near Paddington this morning, there was something different about him.
SHIRLEY	Yes, you're right. There was something different about him. Very different.

Unit 36 p 82

Exercise 3

SUSAN	Is the fish good here?
BERNARD	Yes, it is. And it's always a different kind of fish. Ah. Here's the waiter. How are you today, Tony?
TONY	Fine, thanks. How are you?
BERNARD	Fine, thanks.
TONY	Good. Can I have your order?
SUSAN	Yes, I think I'd like the fish, please. What kind of fish have you got today?
TONY	Oh, I'm sorry. There's no fish today.
BERNARD	No fish?
TONY	No, I'm sorry.
SUSAN	Oh, well then, I think I'd like… Hmm. Oh, dear. I'm not sure now what I'd like.
TONY	Perhaps you'd like a little more time to look at the menu?
BERNARD	Yes, that's a good idea.

TONY	Would you like something to drink?
SUSAN	Yes, uh… there's no fish so… I think I'd like a glass of red wine, please.
BERNARD	Yes, and I'd like a glass of red wine too, please.

Unit 38 p 86

Exercise 3

SUSAN	Larry says he's from Liverpool, but he wasn't born there.
BERNARD	Oh? Where was he born?
SUSAN	In Manchester.
BERNARD	Really? I was born in Manchester, too.
SUSAN	I know. You told me. Larry is forty years old.
BERNARD	Oh… so he's my age.
SUSAN	Yes. His birthday is October the third.
BERNARD	October the third. But that's my birthday.
SUSAN	Yes. Your secretary told me. I talked to her this morning. Bernard, what was your mother's name?
BERNARD	My mother's name?
SUSAN	Yes. Your secretary didn't know that.
BERNARD	My mother's name was Barbara. Why?
SUSAN	Did you know her?
BERNARD	No, she died when I was very young.
SUSAN	She died when you were very young?
BERNARD	Yes.
SUSAN	How old were you when she died?
BERNARD	I don't remember. But my father says I was six months old.
SUSAN	Six months old? You were six months old when your mother died? And her name was Barbara?
BERNARD	Yes. Why are you so surprised?
SUSAN	Because Larry Jasper's mother was called Barbara. And she died when he was six months old, too. That's why.

Unit 39 p 88

Exercise 2

SHIRLEY	Do you know Basil Newton, Tony?
TONY	Who? Basil Newton?
SHIRLEY	Yes, do you know him?
TONY	I know his daughter. But I don't know him.
JACK	How much money did Larry give you?
TONY	How much did he give me?
JACK	Yes. You helped him. And he gave you money for your help. He paid you. We know that. How much did he give you?

TONY	Five hundred.
SHIRLEY	Five hundred. He gave you five hundred?
TONY	Yes. He gave me five hundred.
JACK	How much money did Larry get from Basil Newton? Do you know that?
TONY	No.
SHIRLEY	Basil gave Larry fifty thousand for the picture, Tony. He paid him fifty thousand pounds.
TONY	What? But… but all I got was… was five hundred.
SHIRLEY	Yes. Larry got fifty thousand, all you got was five hundred.

Unit 40 p90

Exercise 3

MR W	You say you're a friend of my son?
SUSAN	Yes. My name is Susan Farr, Mr Winter. I'm a journalist. I'd like to ask you a few questions.
MR W	Questions?
SUSAN	Yes. Perhaps you know what happened yesterday.
MR W	Yes, I read it this morning. It's all very strange.
SUSAN	Yes. Very strange. He and Bernard were born in Manchester on the same day in the same year.
MR W	What?
SUSAN	Yes. The man's name is Larry. His mother's name was Barbara.
MR W	Barbara? His mother's name was…
SUSAN	Barbara. Yes. She died when Larry was six months old.
MR W	Six months old? She died when he was… six months old?
SUSAN	Hello? Hello? Mr Winter? Can you hear me?
MR W	Yes. I can hear you. I never…
SUSAN	Is there something you want to tell me, Mr Winter.
MR W	I never told Bernard.
SUSAN	You didn't tell him?
MR W	No, I never told him.
SUSAN	What didn't you tell him, Mr Winter?
MR W	That he had… that he had…
SUSAN	Yes, please go on, Mr Winter. I'm listening.
MR W	I thought it was better if…
SUSAN	Yes? If what, Mr Winter? You thought it was better if…
MR W	If he didn't know. I thought it was better if he didn't know. That's why I never told him…
SUSAN	Yes?
MR W	… that he had a twin brother.

Word list

These words are on the pages below. Plurals are in brackets (). Verbs are in present and past forms.

A

a	6
a few	85
a little	85
a lot of	16
about	6
above	53
accent(s)	46
address(es)	20
afraid	74
after	25
afternoon(s)	16
again	75
age	60
all	14
all right	14
almost	73
also	62
always	42
am/was	25
American	25
an	34
and	6
angry	87
animal(s)	33
another	40
answer(s)	7
any	51
anything	76
April	79
arch(es)	24
are/were	8
art	34
article(s)	34
artist(s)	77
ask/asked	51
at	67
at all	32
ate (see 'eat')	84
Australia	12
autumn(s)	79

B

bad	19
bath(s)	38
bathroom(s)	38
be (see 'am/ are')	66
beautiful	54
because	44
bed(s)	39
bedroom(s)	38
beer	53
before	25
begin/began	73

beginning(s)	81
behind	22
believe/ believed	90
better	86
big	8
bike(s)	47
black	11
blue	11
book(s)	17
boring	89
born	76
bottle(s)	15
bought (see 'buy')	81
boy(s)	50
Brazil	13
bread	33
breakfast(s)	38
brother(s)	50
brown	11
building(s)	30
bus(es)	17
but	8
buy/bought	34

C

café(s)	10
called	62
camera(s)	47
can/could	22
Canada	8
Canadian	46
car(s)	6
cat(s)	33
centre(s)	18
chair(s)	38
champagne	45
change/ changed	65
cheap	37
cheese	14
chicken	82
child	50
children	50
chip(s)	69
church(es)	31
cigarette(s)	53
cinema(s)	42
circle/circled	19
city(ies)	8
class(es)	91
classic	36
classical	33

clerk(s)	68
clock(s)	7
closed	41
cloud(s)	30
cobra(s)	89
coffee	14
cold	78
colour(s)	11
come/came	43
concert(s)	42
conversation(s)	52
cost(s)	17
country(ies)	8
credit card(s)	68
cup(s)	14
cut/cut	72

D

dangerous	88
dark	54
daughter(s)	50
day(s)	11
delicious	82
department store(s)	18
desk(s)	62
detective(s)	30
diary(ies)	62
did (see 'do/did')	81
die/died	77
difference(s)	46
different	46
difficult	66
dinner(s)	39
do/did	28
doctor(s)	53
does/did	28
dog(s)	33
dollar(s)	53
door(s)	31
double	69
down	41
drank (see 'drink')	84
drink/drank	39

E

early	63
ear(s)	55
easy	66
eat/ate	38
egg(s)	33
eight	7
eighteen	9

eighty	14
eleven	9
else	74
empty	75
end(s)	81
England	8
English	25
enough	66
evening(s)	16
every	81
everything	91
exact	10
example(s)	85
excellent	82
excuse me	10
exercise(s)	53
expensive	36
expert(s)	34
explain/ explained	64
extra	7
eye(s)	78

F

face(s)	36
fair	54
false	91
familiar	76
family(ies)	50
far	9
fat	54
father(s)	50
few	85
fifteen	9
fifth	24
fifty	11
film(s)	36
find/found	53
fine	20
finish/ finished	43
first	24
fish	33
five	7
flat(s)	28
floor(s)	28
food	32
football	35
for	14
forget/forgot	65
form(s)	85
forty	114
four	7
fourteen	9
fourth	24

France	13
French	15
Friday(s)	43
friend(s)	42
from	12
fruit	33
full	75
future	63

G

gave (see 'give')	88
German	15
Germany	13
get/got	52
get up/got up	42
girl(s)	50
give/gave	44
glass(es)	15
go/went	42
golf	35
good	20
good afternoon	20
good morning	21
good night	21
goodbye	21
got (see 'get')	46
green	11
grey	54
ground	
floor(s)	28

H

had (see 'have')	81
hair	54
half past	11
hand(s)	58
happen/ happened	67
happy	78
has/had	63
have/had	63
have to/had to	74
he	13
hear/heard	40
heavier	61
hello	6
help/helped	68
her	23
here	19
him	41
his	23
Holland	78

home(s)	64
hospital(s)	88
hotel(s)	16
hour(s)	11
house(s)	6
how	82
how are you?	20
how many	17
how much	14
hundred	14
hungry	80
husband(s)	51

I

I	13
I'd	44
idea(s)	60
if	72
ill	82
in	8
in front of	19
infinitive(s)	87
information	86
interested	34
interesting	78
interview/ interviewed	65
into	58
Ireland	8
irregular	81
is/was	25
it	13
Italian	15
Italy	13

J

Japan	13
Japanese	15
jazz	42
job(s)	34
journalist(s)	34
just	64

K

key(s)	68
kind of	14
kitchen(s)	38
knew (see 'know')	89
know/knew	35

L

lamb	82
last (week)	76
last name(s)	20
late	63

Longman Group Limited,
Longman House, Burnt Mill, Harlow,
Essex CM20 2JE, England
and Associated Companies
throughout the world.

© Longman Group Ltd 1995
All rights reserved; no part of this publication may be
reproduced, stored in a retrieval system, or transmitted
in any form or by any means, electronic, mechanical,
photocopying, recording, or otherwise without the prior
written permission of the Publishers.

First published 1995

Project Management by Trojan Horse
Publishing, London N1 7RE.
Designed by Gregor Arthur, Trojan Horse.
Cover designed by Claire Sleven.

Illustrated by: Johanna Fernihough
(photomontages), Neil Gower, Val Hill,
Nick Maland, Jenny Ridley (computer graphics),
Helen Tabor ('The Woman with Green Eyes').

Acknowledgements
The author would like to thank Sam Toirac for
his many valuable insights.

We are grateful to the following for permission
to reproduce copyright photos:

Allsport for pages 24b, 43; Robert Harding
Picture Library for 24t, 50ml; Rebecca
Horsewood for 161, 50; Longmans/Trevor
Clifford for 11; Chas Wilder for 15, 23t, 33, 73,
75, 94; Telegraph Colour Library for 19, 31,
42bl, 42tr, 50, 89t.

All other photos by Gareth Boden/Longmans.

We are grateful to the following for their help
with the commissioned photography:
Matthew Baker; Laura Bangert; Boots the
Chemists; British Telecommunications; Blue
Triangle Buses; Briggens House Hotel; Burnt
Mill School; Cafe Flo; Churchgate Street Hotel;
Harlow Playhouse; Dipika Parmer Jenkins; Le
Chat Noir Gallery, Mayfair, London; The Manor
of Groves Hotel; The Mill, Little Hallingbury,
Herts; Nevada Bobs, Harlow, Essex; Our Price;
The Paradise Garage; The Rivers Hospital; H.
Samuels, Watchmakers and Jewellers; St Johns
Arts and Recreation Centre, Old Harlow, Essex;
Constable Taylor, Hertfordshire Constabulary.

Typeset by Trojan Horse Publishing,
London N1 7RE.
Colour Repro by Jade Reprographics,
Braintree, Essex.
Printed in Madrid by Mateu Cromo.

ISBN 0582 254191